ARAB CHRISTIANITY AND JERUSALEM

Arab Christianity and Jerusalem

A History of the Arab Christian Presence in the Holy City

Dr Raouf Abujaber

GILGAMESH
PUBLISHING LTD

Arab Christianity and Jerusalem

Published by Gilgamesh Publishing in 2012
Email: info@gilgamesh-publishing.co.uk
www.gilgamesh-publishing.co.uk

ISBN 978-1-908531-16-2

© Dr Raouf Abujaber 2012

Translated by Hani Rohi Al-Khatib

Printed and bound in the UK by the MPG Books Group, Bodmin and King's Lynn

CIP Data: A catalogue for this book is
available from the British Library

TABLE OF CONTENTS

Foreword

"Walahi!" [By my God!] – A deep yet almost shrill voice behind us shattered more than 400 years' elegant silence in Oxford's Old Palace! My startled Harvard team – up to that sudden prayerful exclamation – had been quietly measuring and carefully affixing 19th-century photographs to 16th-century walls. Turning, we found a stalwart gentleman vigorously pointing at details of Amman's amphitheatre and Jerash's colonnades so as to quiz us about dates we had given to Bonfils photographs. We explained that our chronological estimates derived from interviews conducted above Clermont-Ferrand with octogenarian grandchildren of Félix Bonfils as well as from internal clues (such as Astrakhan caps and kaftans worn by Circassian refugees from Tsarist pogroms evaluating the safety of Transjordanian lands offered to them by the Sultan in 1870).

This, our dramatic first direct encounter with Dr Abujaber, (known to his friends as Abu-Ziad to honour the birth of his elder son), took place in 1980 as we had been gathered together by Prince al-Hassan bin Talal at his alma mater, Christ Church, to share discoveries and puzzles of the Bilad-al-Sham's long and complex history.

Having excavated in Jordan since 1962 while still a student in German universities, I was familiar with Abu-Ziad's family name: his close relatives had served the Hashemite Kingdom as Ministers of State – especially for Economics, Foreign Affairs and, more relevantly, for Tourism and Antiquity. Most relevantly, Abu-Ziad himself had been silently blessed each evening by weary, dusty and thirsty archaeologists – as we imbibed his cooling Amstel, today still heartily brewed with its original Netherlands recipe.

Originally from Nablus, near the homeland of the Samaritans, the Abujabers reintroduced agriculture to the Transjordanian steppe lands in the 1860s – to discover that, after many centuries of lying fallow, their vast fields grew fresh grain so very abundantly that their family records include quite astonishing statistics.

Abu-Ziad himself had, as a businessman, excelled not only in brewing but also in establishing Jordan Dairies and a complex of insurance companies as well as in serving as Governor for Rotary International throughout the Middle East. As a diplomat, Dr Abujaber's career involved some 60 years of service with the Dutch: 35 years as Consul General and decades of delicate advice including his wise personal assistance in establishing Dutch Embassies throughout the region. Knight Commander of the Orange-Nassau Order, Abu-Ziad's ancestral fortress of Yadouda halted the furthest north-westerly advance of the black banners of the Ikhwan from Arabia in the 1920s.

Today, those mighty walls resting atop Bronze Age foundations and displaying the Greek crosses chiselled by centuries of pilgrims, surround a family enterprise called Kan Zaman ("Once upon a time…") where tourists from Queen Alia International Airport can safely sample traditional Bedouin roasted lambs!

It was nearby land, bought to help a cousin overcome a financial crisis, that changed Abu-Ziad's life: that plot had abruptly earned so very much from simply lying on the path of the Airport's runway-expansion that Abu-Ziad became indignant! His decades of ingenious efforts to earn profits resourcefully yet honestly were outstripped by those scrubby, unproductive fields! Passing on his economic responsibilities to his sons with the promise to review their efforts every few months, Abu-Ziad flew to Pembroke College, Oxford – beside the Old Palace across the street from Christ Church. There his brilliant dissertation on the Reagricuturalization of Transjordan made use of multiplex Ottoman tax and military records and especially his own families' much more reliable harvest accounts.

Once formally inducted into "the ancient brotherhood of scholars", Dr Abujaber has gone on to produce dynastic histories, on the Aujaber, Bisharat, Kawar and Seikaly clans as well as his 2005 *Beyond the River* where he brilliantly presented – together with Felicity Cobbing, their Curator – invaluable 19th-century photographs of the Palestine Exploration Fund.

The Abujaber Palace (with its Italianate décor) in Al-Salt, Jordan's first

8

capital, has been taken over by the State as a museum. Nearby, the Latin (i.e. "Roman") Catholic Church is still known in Al-Salt as the Abujaber Church and daily reminds Saltis of the family's generosity and faith over a century and a half ago.

Sheikh of the steppe land, the farmer, the brewer, the dairyman, the economist, the international organizer and diplomat, is also a linguist – acquainted with Ottoman Turkish as well as French, Dutch and multiple dialects of Arabic. Surely no one so variously equipped has ever attempted to write such a broadly embracive and humanly poignant chronicle of intricate history and constantly martyred humanity.

Dr Abujaber's command of sources ranges from oral anecdotes of kinsmen (including hereditary Commissioners for Tsars' educational subsidies to Christian schools) and even to excerpts he has chosen from (once unified) Jerusalem's 1940s telephone directories which directly attest to the occupational diversity and urban spread of Christian families throughout the space of today's tragically segmented Holy City.

"Roma viduta, Fide perduta" ("Once you see Rome, you lose your faith") could also be applied, sadly, to squabbles – indeed, periodically, outright monastic battles – among Jerusalemite Christians. Dr Abujaber presents his enthralling story without painting over blemishes. In particular, for recent years, his chronicle is illuminated by his personal involvement in the anguishing deposition of a corrupt alien Patriarch found to be selling to Israelis (via legalistic chicanery and "straw men" as agents) Arab properties that had been piously bequeathed to the Church by members of Jerusalemite families.

Yet this loving, if at times heartbreaking, account of Christianity's birthplace is permeated by the same profound faith and dedication to truthfulness epitomized in the first word we heard from him: "Walahi!"

May God smile upon that robust faithfulness of his, upon his readers, and upon that sacred space called "City of Peace" for 35 centuries at least or, even more simply and poignantly, in Arabic "al-Quds" ("the Holy").

Dr Carney Gavin (Catholic Priest)

Former Curator of the Harvard Semitic Museum.

Introduction

It is natural that relations between Christians and Jerusalem go back to the period when Jesus started preaching his message. It is confirmed that Christian existence in the Holy City remained continuous from that time with the exception of a sixty-year period starting when the Jews rebelled against the Roman state in AD 70. Then, Bishop Sam'aan (Simon) who wanted to protect the Christians from any potential harm moved with them to the city of Pela – known now as Tabaqat Fahel – in the Northern Ghawr east of the River Jordan opposite the city of Beisan (Skythopolis of the Decapolis). Thus they escaped the sufferings of those inhabitants who stayed in Jerusalem.

Titus, the Roman general, laid siege to Jerusalem in AD 70 and destroyed it completely. The city stayed in ruins for sixty years, after which Emperor Hadrian built a completely new city on its ruins and named it Aelia. After that the Christian faithful returned to the city where they resettled and elected bishops from among them to run the affairs of their church.

The city underwent turbulent times from that period until AD 638, when the city surrendered to Muslim armies led by Caliph Omar. Jerusalem's Arab Christian inhabitants started to live peacefully side by side along their brethren Muslim Arabs while other Christian factions such as Greeks, Assyrians, Armenians, Abyssinians, Copts, Kurj (Georgians) and, at later stages, Europeans who came with the Crusades, all started to live within the city depending on circumstances. It is confirmed, however, that the Omari covenant (Uhdah Al-Umarayyah) which was signed and delivered by Caliph Omar to Patriarch Sophronius in AD 638, provided a new turn in the lives of Arab Christians within the city and allowed Romans to leave. That is why Romans were not mentioned in Arab history books written during the 7th and 8th centuries, which discussed events that occurred in the Holy Land during the Umayyad and Abbasid rules. Those books discussed in detail the bloody battles that raged on the northern borders between the Arabs and the Byzantines ending with the start of the Crusades.

It is with this turbulent background in mind, and at a time when the Arab nation finds itself deeply involved with a new situation in the Holy City, that I have decided to write about life in Jerusalem during the last two hundred years. I found it most important, rather imperative, that I put on record, the events in Jerusalem during the upheaval that started with the outstanding advance of the Egyptian Expeditionary Force under Ibrahim Pasha, his period of ten years of Egyptian Reforms, followed by the Tanzimat era (Ottoman Reform) of Sultan Abdulmajid I (1839-61). These two hundred years were truly a great change in the life of the holiest of cities and I am grateful that I have been given the energy and time to write its history. The diversity and complexity of the subject matter drawn upon in this research made it difficult at times to be accurate about dates of events in the Christian calendar. It was found more suitable not to be overly strict, trusting that the reader will take this into consideration.

Our knowledge and awareness about events in the Holy Land during the last two hundred years will, beyond doubt, support our basic stands, Muslims and Christians alike, in defending our holy places and preserving the Arab identity of Jerusalem and its freedom for the coming generations, and the interests of humanity, at large.

Raouf Abujaber

CHAPTER I

General Conditions in Jerusalem
Early 19th century (1800-1831)

In the early part of the 19th century, Palestine – like other parts of Bilad al-Sham – lived under Ottoman rule. Jerusalem and its villages were a part of the Wilayat (governorate) of Akko (Acre) whose governor, Ahmad Pasha al-Jazzar, successfully drove off Napoleon's troops from the city's walls in 1798. The period from the death of Sheikh Dhaher al-'Umar al-Zaydani in 1775[1] to al-Jazzar's death in 1804[2] was a critical era marked by many uprisings and internal wars. The result was the impoverishment of the inhabitants and the destruction of a land which had enjoyed prosperity just fifty years before that. It was at this time that Volney, the famous French voyager, made his trip to Egypt and Syria and recorded his sightings during the years 1783 to 1785 in a book which was translated into English and published in two parts in 1787.

According to Volney, Jerusalem's population at the time of his visit was between 12,000 and 14,000. Although he does not mention the number of Christians in the city, his reference to Christian sects mentions that the official responsible for collecting taxes and duties in the city faced considerable problems as a result of feuds between the Christian inhabitants.

To understand this, we have to know that there were many Christian factions: Orthodox, Latin, Armenians, Copts, Abyssinians and, at the later stage, Catholics.

Each sect was envious of the holy places possessed by the others, and each tried to outdo the other in trying to bribe Ottoman governors to gain their support. Each sect sought to gain extra privileges at the expense of rivals and each was more than willing to betray any mistake committed by another sect, such as, for example, repairing a church without a permit or allowing a parade to exceed the time permitted or even permitting a visiting pilgrim to enter through the wrong gate.

All these complaints were gladly received by the government, which used them to its advantage, while officials also benefited from the bribes. This mutual hatred and the futile conflicts between the various monasteries and their followers worked to the Turks' advantage and provided the opportunity to generate good profits. It was not, then, in their interests to see an end to these conflicts.

The city's revenues officially exceeded 100,000 girsh (piasters) annually (about 4,000 gold guineas). Each pilgrim paid a ten girsh entrance fee and the same amount to visit the River Jordan.

In addition each monastery and convent paid an annual designated amount in addition to the bribes paid to the official for allowing export of souvenirs purchased by the pilgrims. These exports totaled more than three hundred crates of rosary beads, icons, crosses, embroideries and figurines, made from coral, wood, silk, pearls, gold and silver. This trade earned the monasteries more than 100,000 girsh annually for goods exported to Turkey, Italy, Portugal and, foremost, Spain.

Production and sale of those souvenirs profited Muslim and Christian inhabitants alike.

Pilgrims' visits provided another important source of revenue. The number of visiting Westerners was relatively low, but Eastern Pilgrims coming from Greece, the Greek Isles, Anatolia, Armenia, Egypt and Syria were great in number and exceeded 2,000 in 1784, each paying at least 4,000 girsh while many spent more than 60,000 girsh each on alms and vows. Monks' records show the number of pilgrims in previous years amounted to 10-12,000 annually.[3]

Volney touches on the existence of Catholics in Jerusalem and says that Franks (Western Europeans) owned the Saint Sauveur Monastery in Jerusalem which ranked first in importance among Holy Land missions in the Ottoman Empire and had seventeen Franciscan monks of various nationalities, although mostly French, Italian and Spanish. The head of the administration of the monastery had to be Italian while his deputy had to be French. The head abbot had to be Spanish.

Each had a key to the safe and any money spent had to be approved by all three. Twenty years earlier, according to Volney, they had run out of money, so they appealed to the King of Spain who considered himself the protector of all Christian missions in the East. He provided them with more than 30,000 gold guineas to back Catholic activities in Jerusalem and all corners of Palestine.[4]

Even though Jerusalem had a life different from other cities because of its religious stature, it was nonetheless directly affected by prevailing conditions in other areas of Palestine, especially the central areas. The contributions made by pilgrims visiting the Holy Land were vital to the local economy in Jerusalem, but depended on the safety and security of all parts of the land. The farmers in the mountains around Jerusalem relied for their livelihood on selling their crops and produce in Jerusalem's markets.

One story worth mentioning in this period is when Mohammad Pasha Abu Maraq, the ex-governor of Jaffa, noted that the Pilgrimage (Hajj) Route to the Hejaz was closed for three years following the death of Al-Jazzar. He convinced the Ottoman State to appoint him as Wali (governor) of Jaffa, Gaza, Ramlah, Lidda and Jerusalem for the purpose of opening the route for Hajj caravans from Gaza and Via Ma'an. He arrived in Jaffa in early1806 and settled in the city forgetting his earlier promises to open the Hajj caravan route. His tenure was marked by injustice and corruption and he made the lives of his subjects miserable. He closed the road that led Christian visitors to Jerusalem and rerouted them via Ramallah where he burdened them with all sorts of heavy taxes and levies. He had his underlings extort *baksheesh* and kickbacks, resulting in a decline in the number of Christian visitors to Jerusalem, Ramlah and Jaffa. They complained to Suleiman Pasha, Wali of Akko (Acre) and later to the central government in Constantinople (Istanbul) which lead the Sultan to reprimand and censure Mohammad Pasha Abu Maraq.When he refused to comply he was removed from his position and later, in early 1807, he was sentenced to death by beheading. Surrounded in Jaffa, he successfully fled to Egypt where he sought the help from the Wali there, Muhammad Ali Pasha, who promised to intercede on his behalf with the Sultanate in Istanbul.[5]

Shrines in Jerusalem, especially the Holy Sepulchre were, and still are, the core of the conflict between various sects in the city. During this period disputes were getting worse between the Greek Orthodox and the Armenians. When fire broke out within the Holy Sepulchre early on

Wednesday, 30 September 1808 and continued for two whole days, most of Jerusalem's Christians saw it as a major catastrophe, not only because of the physical damage but because of the suspicions they started to have that the Armenians were behind it, driven by their ambition to have a larger role in supervising the church. The noted Palestinian historian 'Aref al-'Aref quoted Reverend Michael Brek al-Dimashqi's claim that the fire started within the Church of the Holy Sepulchre at the hands of the Armenians. Others also claimed that it was arson although there were also those who refuted this theory.

The barriers that stood in the way of restoring the church showed that the rift between the sects was much deeper than had been thought. The Latins (Catholics) were also waiting for the first opportunity to strengthen their own position and to gain more privileges. When the Greek Orthodox succeeded in obtaining a *faraman* (decree) from Sultan Mahmud II (1808–1839) allowing them to rebuild the church after the fire, the Latins and Armenians objected, delaying restoration work until 4 August 1809. Seventy days later they complained to the Sultan about the Greek Orthodox sect. The Sultan formed a committee of seven *qadis* (judges) headed by Sheikh al-Islam, the chief justice, to look into the matter. Once each party had submitted its documents the committee ruled that only the Greek Orthodox sect had the right to restore the building of the burnt church. The Sultan affirmed the decision, decreeing that only the Greek Orthodox should commence restoration works against which no other party would be allowed to object and that the building should be restored to its pre-fire state without any additions. He also decreed that the Armenians should go back to their own spaces within the church after restoration work had been completed and that their lanterns and chandeliers were to be returned to the same spots they had occupied before the fire.

The Copts followed suit and demanded to rebuild their tiny chapel which stood at the back of the Holy Sepulchre. Their request was turned down and the Greek Orthodox started rebuilding it, smaller than it used to be, in order to widen the path around the Tomb.[6] Restoration work continued until the end of the year when the Janissaries who had acted as guards, were stood down. They were driven out of Jerusalem by Abdallah Pasha al-Azem, the governor of Damascus, during his visit to Jerusalem and replaced with regular troops. After he left, the Janissaries revolted – encouraged by the Armenians – and attacked the Church of the Holy

Sepulchre, killing a master sculptor, wounding a number of labourers and demolishing the building. They looted all the churches and chapels. The governor of Damascus reacted by sending seven hundred Moroccan soldiers led by their chief, Abu Dhuray'a, who entered the city early on the morning of 10 January, 1810 and crushed the revolt killing all the insurgents.[7] After that, restoration work resumed, coming to a final total of 355,000 riyals. The new Holy Sepulchre building was inaugurated on 13 September 1810 after which the Latin and Armenian communities were regarded as partners of the Greek Orthodox community in supervising the Holy Tomb.

The old conflicts between the various Christian sects which had surfaced anew during the battle of how to rebuild the Church of the Holy Sepulchre serve as an example of how extreme national feeling can hide behind religious practices. Along the same lines must be noted the dispute between the Orthodox and the Armenians who used to celebrate Easter together until 1633 when the Armenians decided (as quoted in the "Summary of the History of the Jerusalem Orthodox Church") to celebrate alone by having their own holiday on Light Saturday inside the Church of the Holy Sepulchre. Such disputes and conflicts were, at the same time, a sign of the corruption that reigned supreme during Ottoman rule with officials using such conflicts to obtain gifts, bribes and the best jobs, abusing their authority and influencing the government in Constantinople through the clerics and diplomats accredited there. It is noted that this battle, like the ones before and after, was between the monks who controlled the patriarchates and monasteries, and who were of different nationalities (chiefly from Greece, Armenia, France, Italy and Spain) while the Arabs of different Christian denominations played no significant role except to raise their voices whenever they were urged to do so to support one or other sect who felt their holy places and shrines were being attacked.

There is another important observation here, which is the Ottoman insistence on obtaining a permit from the highest government echelons before doing any repairs or restoration work to any Christian buildings and shrines, and also insisting on certain technical specifications that should not be exceeded. Residents had no choice but compliance.

A new development affecting Christian status in the Holy Land took place, especially in Jerusalem, at the start of the 19th century. Russia started to show more interest in the Holy Land and Jerusalem after the evaporation of Napoleon's threat. It saw a golden opportunity in 1814 when Polikarius, the Patriarch of Jerusalem (1808-1827) submitted a complaint to Tsar Alexander I alleging that hostile acts were being directed against the Orthodox causing great damage and a lot of concern. The accusation was, in fact, directed against Catholic activities which were backed by the French. In reaction, the Tsar ordered his accredited Ambassador in Constantinople to submit a protest to the sultan.

The French violations of the agreed rights were something that the Greeks took very seriously. Each party felt that it was protected by its national state. In 1817 the Sultan issued a decree confirming the status quo, yet complaints against Catholic violations continued.

Russian officials started to notice the difficulties that Russian pilgrims were facing while visiting the Holy Land and observed that their lack of protection placed them at the mercy of both the Turks and the Greeks. As a result Russia established its first consulate in the Holy Land, basing it in Jaffa since it was the port of entry for Russians arriving in Palestine.

This was probably the start of the period where Russia came to be seen as the "Protector" of the Orthodox community throughout the Ottoman Empire.[8] At the same time the war of liberation against the Turkish occupation started in Greece. Both Muslim and Ottoman residents in Jerusalem began to look at the order of Fraternity of the Holy Sepulchre in a hostile manner. This hostile feeling was soon directed at all Orthodox Christians and a new wave of persecution started. The Christians were forced to wear black turbans and some of them were imprisoned, charged with supporting Greek liberation movements. Many fled to neighbouring areas. One 20th-century historian writing in detail about the sad situation noted:

> History remembers that injustice and punishments inflicted on the Orthodox Christians were very severe throughout Palestine, especially in Acre where they were forced to wear nothing but black and violators were thrown in jail. Persecution reached high levels in Damascus and Jerusalem. Muslims did not act, however, without having been encouraged by other Christian sects and also the Jews, especially in Jerusalem, for the Jews were noted for their slyness and the Armenians were driven by old frictions and by their wish to lay their hands on more shrines.[9]

These persistent difficulties had a significant impact on the daily life of the Orthodox Christian community, but came to seem normal for the other three major sects: Greek Orthodox, the Latins and the Armenians with side participations of Abyssinians, Copts, Assyrians and Kurj, all at a time when the Protestant world started for the first time to express interest in Jerusalem, where it had not previously had any activities.

In 1819 two US missionaries, Levy Parsons and Pliny Fisk, were sent from New York to Jerusalem to establish a base for missionary work. Parsons became the first Protestant missionary to set foot in Jerusalem and to work among Eastern Churches and Jews[10]. The motive behind the move was primarily to spread the Gospel among nations to strengthen their faith, but it was also a response to prevailing 19th-century concepts of Christ's imminent Second Coming – something that was to impel Christians to work hard and fast to spread the Bible across the globe in line with their perception of Christ's will and testament.[11] Historian Khalil Qazaqya disagrees, however, and mentions a different date stating:

> In 1822 the first Protestant Missionaries arrived in Jerusalem and were followers of Calvin. They started by spreading loads of different books and pamphlets among the residents with intent of spreading their brand of faith believing the Holy Land was fertile to accept ideologies and faiths. Those books were in all languages, especially Hebrew. Their first missionary was Joseph Wolf who was a Jew who converted to Christianity. He took residence within the American Monastery and worked really hard until he succeeded in laying a foundation for the Protestant sect in Palestine.[12]

During this period, two important developments occurred, both of which were to attack the life of Jerusalem and its residents. The first was the start of the arrival of Russian visitors in great numbers. The second was the Greek liberation from the Ottoman yoke, as earlier mentioned. The importance of both developments and how they affected Jerusalem, Palestine and the whole area was perceived differently from one person to another. Both occurred just a short time before the start of the Egyptian mandate over Bilad al-Sham, a mandate which lasted for ten eventful years.

Qazaqya mentions that Russian visitors started arriving in the Holy Land in 1811. Their numbers were small in the beginning but by 1819 as many as two hundred were escorted by a Russian nobleman called Dashkov who toured all the Holy Land before settling on 20 September of the same year (his arrival was probably in March, just before Easter). Before returning home, Dashkov appointed a Greek man holding Russian citizenship as the accredited Russian consul in Palestine, to be based in Jaffa. His responsibilities included looking after the safety and well-being of Russian visitors. Since the Russians did not have any property in Palestine at the time he resided within the Greek Orthodox monastery. This was not looked at favourably by other Christian sects. This also strengthened the government's doubts about him and the Greek Orthodox monks especially against the backdrop of the 1821 Greek rebellion against the Ottoman Empire.[13] Hopwood mentions that the first Russian Consular Centre was established in Jaffa in 1820 and that the rising interest of Russia in Syria made the Russian Foreign Ministry move the consulate from Jaffa to Beirut, becoming the base of the Russian Consulate for both Syria and Palestine. Its first objective was to establish good relations with the Orthodox Patriarch and the Church Authorities in Syria and Palestine while also serving local religious interests and paying exceptional attention to the welfare of the Eastern Church, something which was always a priority for the Tsar. Also of importance was maintaining good relations with the heads of other Christian sects and assisting Russian pilgrims visiting the Holy Land.[14]

Meanwhile the Greek War of Liberation had started in 1821, following the formation by Greek patriots of a revolutionary society in Vienna called Heneri ("fraternity") which established schools and spread the sciences among the Greek communities. Simultaneously, they had created a secret society carrying the same name but with purely political objectives, i.e. to wrest independence for Greece from Ottoman rule. At first it was based in Odessa in the Crimea but it then moved to Kiev in the Ukraine – both areas under Ottoman rule at the time. Both locations gave credibility to the belief that forming the society was done at the urging of Alexander I, the Russian Tsar who started internal agitation within the Ottoman State with the goal of fulfilling the will of Peter the Great to turn Constantinople into the Gate ("Key") of the Russian Kingdom.[15] More than 20,000 young men joined the society in the Al-Moura area and they started attacking forts and citadels. It gained strength and was able in August 1822 to defeat Khorshid Pasha's army in the Battle of Thermopily. The event was preceded by Greek mariners' success in setting the Turkish fleet (Donanmeh) on fire at the port of Sagz Island, slaying 3,000 of its mariners on 18 June 1822. The courage and bravery of the Greeks were much lauded by the Europeans, who started forming societies to support what they were doing. Some, such as Lord Byron, the famous English poet, actually joined the Greeks.[16]

These events inevitably resulted in every Greek residing within the Ottoman Empire being viewed with some doubt by local authorities. In Jerusalem, Ottoman officials treated the monks of the Holy Land Fraternity with scepticism and hostility and looted all their money and possessions, driving them to borrow money at exorbitant rates of interest. A new wave of suppression and oppression started against Christians. Quite aside from being forced to wear black turbans, many were thrown into jail and had to pay hefty ransoms to gain their freedom. These harsh conditions, coupled with the levy of a war tax, led to a state of general chaos. In 1824 Christians and Muslims alike rebelled against the injustices that were prevalent. When the government sent troops to punish them, many fled to other parts of Palestine, hiding their furniture and other belongings inside the monasteries of Mar Elias, Al-Musallaba, and others. Government troops looted and took control of the monasteries. The Armenians seized the opportunity to take over the Cemetery of Zion.

Those appalling conditions lasted for the next seven years and did not cease until the Greeks gained their independence once the Ottoman and Egyptian fleets were destroyed at the hands of British, French and Russian navies at the Battle of Navarin on 20 October 1827. The Egyptian army was forced to retreat from Greece on 3 September 1828.[17]

The monks of the Fraternity of the Holy Sepulchre had to suffer all kinds of hardships, economic and otherwise. Because of the decrease in numbers of visitors, they could not even pay the wages of the sentries at the doors of the Holy Sepulchre. When their debts reached 30 million piastres, Patriarch Athanasios V (1827-1845) who had been elected in Constantinople, tried very hard to settle this debt. He was aided by Patriarch Constantine who petitioned Sultan Mahmud in 1832 asking him to levy a tax of one piastre on every Orthodox living within the Ottoman Empire.

The Sultan agreed to the petition and also donated 500,000 piastres (girsh), a sum that was matched by the Prince of Serbia. The patriarch was able, through his delegates and emissaries who travelled throughout the

Orthodox world and through the donation box in all Orthodox churches, to collect large sums of money that enabled him to pay all the debts in instalments as agreed with Muhammad Ali Pasha, the Wali of Egypt, in 1832 after the Egyptian Army occupied Bilad Al-Sham (Great Syria)[18] and took over its administration.

Notes:

(1) Tawfiq Mu'ammar Dhaher al-'Umar, *Nazareth*, 1979, p.249

(2) Hayder Ahmad al-Shihabi, *History of Ahmad Pasha al-Jazzar*, Librarie Antoine, Beirut, 1955, p.506

(3) M.C-F. Volney, *Travels through Syria and Egypt: In the years 1783, 1784l, and 1785. Containing the Present Natural and Political State of Those Countries, their Productions, Arts, Manufactures, and Commerce, with Observations on the Manners, Customs, and Government of the Turks and Arabs*, 2 vols., 2nd ed. (London: Printed for G.G.J. and J. Robinson, 1788), pp.304-309.

(4) Ibid, pp.313-317

(5) Ibrahim al-'Aura, *History of Soleiman Pasha al-'Adel Dayr*, Al-Mukhalis Press 1936, p.16

(6) Shehadeh Khoury and Nicola Khoury, *Summary of the History of the Jerusalem Orthodox Church*, Beit Al-Maqdis Press, 1925, p.180

(7) Inkishariyya (Janissaries), a Turkish word meaning "The New Military Force" that, until the 17th Century were from amongst the Christians of Ottoman Empire. After that, they became a special army that misbehaved. Sultan Mahmud II (1808-1939) dissolved them and destroyed their establishment and quarters after killing many of them.

(8) Derek Hopwood, *The Russian Presence in Syria and Palestine, 1843-1914: Church and Politics in the Near East* (Oxford: Clarendon Press, 1969) pp.13-15

(9) Khalil Ibrahim Qazaqya, *History of the Jerusalem Church*, Al-Muqtataf & Muyatam, Cairo 1924, p.154

(10) Rafiq Farah, *A History of the Anglican Church in Jerusalem 1841-1991* (Jerusalem) 1995, part 1, p.64

21

(11) Ibid, p.62

(12) Qazaqya, *History of the Jerusalem Church*, p.154

(13) Ibid, p.153

(14) Hopwood, *The Russian Presence in Syria and Palestine, 1843-1914*, p.15

(15) Muhamad Farid, *Tarikh Al-Dawla Al-'Aliya Al-'Othmaniya*, Dar Al-Jeel, Beirut 1977, pp.206-209

(16) Khoury & Khoury, *Summary History of the Orthodox Church Of Jerusalem*, p.187

(17) Muhamad Farid *Tarikh Al-Dawla Al-'Aliya Al-'Othmaniya*, Dar Al-Jeel, Beirut 1977, p.218

(18) Khoury & Khoury, *Summary History of the Orthodox Church Of Jerusalem*, p.156

CHAPTER II

Period of Egyptian Rule in
Bilad Al-Sham (1831-1841)

The relations and dealings of Muhammad Ali Pasha, the Wali (governor) of Egypt, with the Sultan and other Walis within the Ottoman Sultanate did not distract his attention from the internal affairs of the country. Since his appointment by the Sultan on 8 July 1805 he started work to improve the country's infrastructure: building canals, schools, factories and workshops. In order to carry out his programmes he had to levy steep taxes and use forced labour to provide the manpower for his huge projects. This drove large numbers of Egyptians to emigrate to Bilad al-Sham, many of whom sought refuge under the umbrella of Abdallah Pasha, the Wali of Akko (Acre). When Muhammad Ali Pasha asked for their return, the Wali of Akko declined the request under the pretext that all were the subjects of one Sultan and had the right to reside anywhere within the Sultanate.[1] The real reason behind the refusal could have been Abdallah Pasha's desire to make use of those peasants' expertise in cotton cultivation.

This feud, in addition to Muhammad Ali Pasha's desire for independence and to ensure future rule of Egypt exclusively for his descendants, as well as his dream of grabbing Syria from the Turks and annexing it to Egypt and declaring total independence from the Ottoman State,[2] all led to the arrival of the Egyptian campaign led by Ibrahim Pasha. They succeeded in occupying Jerusalem and other Palestinian cities without any fighting in October 1831 and were able to gain control of the fortified Akko (Acre) on 27 May 1832 after laying siege to it for many months.

23

The campaign went on to occupy all parts of Syria and entered Turkish territory. Following the Kutahia agreement, signed on 5 May 1833, Egyptian armies withdrew to areas beyond the Toros Mountains. As a result, Muhammad Ali Pasha was confirmed as Wali of Egypt for life and was appointed Wali of the four regions of Bilad al-Sham: Acre, Tripoli, Aleppo and Damascus, in addition to the island of Crete. Jerusalem, which before the arrival of the Egyptians had been under the jurisdiction of Abdallah Pasha, the Wali of Acre, suffered under the strict rule of Sheikh Sa'eed al-Mustafa who had followed the orders of Abdallah Pasha strictly, preventing anyone not carrying a "ticket of passage" from entering the city. This caused Jerusalemites to suffer since they were dependent on income from visitors who came to their city from many parts of the world.[3]

During this time a Greek priest named Spirodon was the head of Mar Saba monastery near Bethlehem. He wrote in detail about the events he witnessed in his manuscript *Annals of Palestine 1821-1841*. Although his account was mixed with the views of the Greek Fraternity of the Holy Sepulchre, of which Spirodon was a member, it is nonetheless useful in giving an idea of the thinking of Jerusalemites during these turbulent times.

This historian starts by saying that divine intervention helped to correct the injustices in Jerusalem as God punished Abdallah Pasha for the many mistakes he committed in persecuting the Greek Orthodox community, giving him a taste of his own medicine. His vanity and rudeness made him an enemy of Muhammad Ali Pasha, the Wali of Egypt who sent his son Ibrahim Pasha, just returned from Greece, to fight him. In December 1831 Abdallah Pasha had his domain attacked simultaneously from land and sea. Most of the areas in his governorate were taken without any fighting and he was besieged in Acre and finally driven to seek clemency from Ibrahim Pasha who sent him under guard to Muhammad Ali Pasha in Egypt. The occupation of Acre caused the residents of Jerusalem to celebrate by singing and dancing in every corner and street in the city. For five full days all inhabitants celebrated – Muslims, Greeks, Franks, Armenians and even Jews all expressing their joy and glee since the arrival of the Egyptian army brought freedom with it. Muslims, however, couldn't hide their feelings even while taking part in the celebrations – they anticipated the changes Egypt would seek under the pretext of reform. Already they started witnessing things they hated; regular troops wearing western-style tight trousers and carrying modern weapons while playing musical instruments – exactly in the style of Europeans.

The monk moves on from the political stage to economic matters. 1832 was apparently a year of very little rainfall resulting in a sharp increase in prices. The poor suffered and so did the "Fraternity" that used to distribute free bread daily to the poor and desperate within the city. Spirodon, as head of Mar Saba Monastery had to supervise this distribution personally. Among the recipients were 185 men from the Ibaidiyya tribe who were originally from Lazestan, and the story goes that Mar Sab personally interceded on their behalf with Emperor Justinian who pardoned their crimes and bequeathed them to Mar Saba Monastery as guards and slaves to serve and live there. They became Muslims after the keys of the city were handed over to Caliph Omar but they stayed near the monastery.[4] Spirodon mentions that 1832 was the last year for distribution of bread as Ibrahim Pasha stopped the century-old practice which caused long hardship for the monastery. He reports that the monks had some kind of connection with Muhammad Ali Pasha from whom they were granted the right to buy large quantities of grain and rice at the going price and credit.[5]

Spirodon reports how divine grace enabled freedom to emerge when a Russian officer arrived in Jerusalem after Russia's victory over Turkey at Adrianople in Asia. When he noticed how badly visitors were treated during their visit to the Holy Sepulchre, he took the opportunity on his subsequent visit to Egypt to seek audience with Muhammad Ali Pasha and complained to him about the treatment of pilgrims and how they were forced to pay entrance fees and *baksheesh* (tips). He explained to him that Christian Russia would not allow that to continue. In response, according to Spirodon's narrative, Muhammad Ali ordered the cancellation of these fees and stopped their collection by the door guards or the key keepers. He also ordered that the church's doors be kept open at all times. This order was carried by the Armenian Boghos Bey who in turn sent it to the Armenians in Jerusalem who delivered it to the Wali (the governor of Jerusalem). On 13 January 1834, Armenians entered the church through the open doors and with them entered pilgrims from all nations. From that time it became customary that Armenians, Latins and Greeks would open the doors completely.[6]

These narratives, regardless of their biased content at times, give us an idea about the prevailing situation in Jerusalem once Egyptian rule had arrived and highlight the significance of these new freedoms – the opening of the churches' doors and the exemption from paying entrance fees were welcomed with joy, anticipating the arrival of a new era of freedom. There were, however, conflicting views on this era in the history of Syria. Dr Asad Rustum, the noted historian, comments: "it is wrong to assume that Ibrahim Pasha was popular and at the same time considered by many in Syria and Palestine (in 1831) as the saviour." On the contrary, there is enough evidence in the archives to show that he was viewed with disdain and hatred. Ibrahim Pasha himself, in one of his letters to his father dated August 1833, wrote that he knew that the people of Syria and Palestine and Adana were obliged to accept him against their wishes because of the circumstances surrounding them. He complained about the deception and craftiness he faced from the residents of Jerusalem, Nablus, Damascus and Aleppo when he laid siege to Acre. According to him, the only people who deserved his trust and goodwill were Christians and some Druzes in Jebel Lubnana.[7]

It is only fair, however, to mention that Ibrahim Pasha laid the foundation for equal treatment of subjects of different religious sects in Jerusalem. According to estimates, the population in 1835 totalled 10,750; including 4,500 Muslims, 3,250 Christians and 3,000 Jews.[8] He cancelled all previous orders concerning wearing certain colours and restricting modes of riding animals and banned bribery and extortion under any pretext. He also cancelled the *jizyah* (tax levied on non-Muslims) and levied a *kharaj* tax on Christians in return for exemption from military service which was restricted to Muslims and obligatory. He allowed foreigners to trade within his domain and encouraged commerce, agriculture and the soap industry.[9] One of the administrative changes the government of Muhammad Ali Pasha made in Syria was the abolition of the feudal system, reappointing feudal lords to minor administrative positions for a small fraction of the money they used to get before. Later they were to be deposed entirely and others appointed in their places as had happened in Lebanon and Palestine before.[10]

The Egyptians sensed bad things in the air when Ibrahim Pasha heard about the rebellion in the mountains of Nablus and Jerusalem and moved towards Jerusalem. He arrived on Thursday, 12 April 1834 and erected a camp on Mount Zion, entering the city on the second day through King David's Gate and marching to the Haram area where he was given a formal reception with chants and dances. Once he had prayed he apologized for not accepting the invitations to stay at any of the residents' houses. In the afternoon he received delegations that arrived to welcome him, led, as customary, by the Latins then the Greeks, followed by the Armenians. One afternoon before Palm Sunday, he paid a surprise visit to the Holy Sepulchre Church, which was teeming with supplicants from all denominations, accompanied by a small military unit, the Mufti and the caretaker (*mitwalli*). Once he had toured the inside he commented "What a great and beautiful church for Christians".[11]

The manuscript of "Palestine Events" notes that earlier the number of Orthodox pilgrims had rarely exceeded 3,000 annually. Between 1825 and 1834 the Armenians only had 4,000 pilgrims annually. During religious celebrations in the year of Ibrahim Pasha's visit, there were, on Light Saturday at the Holy Sepulchre, 4,000 Orthodox pilgrims plus 2,000 Arab Orthodox from Aleppo, Antioch, Damascus, Beirut and Tripoli, including visitors from Lebanon, both Catholic and Maronite. There were also 2,000 Orthodox who came from Jerusalem itself and from its surrounding villages. In addition the number of Armenians, Copts and Assyrians reached 6,000. Present for the celebration this year was Antonios, the Pope of the Coptic Church accompanied by one of his bishops.

When Ibrahim Pasha, accompanied by 300 soldiers, attended the celebrations on Bright Sunday more than 1,500 worshippers crowded the place, It was hot inside and when the holy light appeared people rushed outside while 500 Arabs and Armenians, who were outside, rushed inside. Many people fell on the ground and were trampled; it was pure bedlam. Ibrahim Pasha was unable to escape and fainted inside the church prompting his escorts to carry him outside where he got his breath back. Once he had drunk some water he gave his orders to organize the evacuation of the area. His troops were able to move the dead and the injured. Deaths among the Orthodox were 27 pilgrims and 16 women and children. The Armenians suffered more than 100 deaths, and the total number of injured exceeded 300 from both sects. Ibrahim Pasha was very saddened by what had occurred; the majority of visitors and pilgrims left the city without celebrating Easter the following day. The Armenians cancelled their Easter celebrations to mourn the victims who had died the previous day.[12]

At the same time, rebellion against Egyptian rule was growing throughout Palestine, prompting Ibrahim Pasha to call for a meeting that included dignitaries from Jerusalem and Nablus. The meeting took place on 25 April, 1834 and he informed those gathered that one in five of all young men were to be recruited into the army and that he was intending to recruit 3,000 youths from both areas including 200 from the city of

Jerusalem.[13] Three days after the meeting the Pasha received urgent news about plague-related deaths within the village of Abu Dis. This made him leave Jerusalem quickly, leaving behind a garrison of 1,000 men. His flight encouraged the crowds of peasants who had gathered around the city walls to attack the city.

As if all that was not enough, the city experienced an earthquake on the morning of Sunday, 13 May 1834. Many houses were destroyed, as well as part of the city wall. Monasteries in Bethlehem were also damaged. The peasants' attacks continued the following day and they were able to breach the walls. Chaos reigned through the city and looting started on a large scale obliging the heads of monasteries to use the services of guards brought from the neighbouring village of Ain Karem to protect the Franciscan monastery. The Greek and Armenian monasteries hired guards from Al-Malha village and from Jerusalem's Muslim communities. Another danger emerged: the plague spread within the Greek Ministry and then across the city. Seven died at the Patriarchate, five in the convent and nine within the Christian Quarter. At the Latins' monastery, eleven monks and six civilians died. Monk Spirodon, the head of Mar Saba Monastery, declared that Jerusalem underwent three ordeals at one time: war, hunger and the plague.[14]

For the Christians these difficult conditions were compounded by the conflicts among their various sects, making their lives very difficult at a time when they could have benefited from the new Egyptian policy of openness towards moderation and diversity, something which had been met favourably by Christians and Jews while angering Muslims.[15] Ibrahim Pasha sent a strict letter of warning to the Muslims responding to accusations from the Christians reporting their mistreatment in spite of the new Egyptian policy of openness. The letter stated:

> You are aware that Jerusalem contains many monasteries, churches and shrines that are visited each year by followers of the Christians and Jewish Faiths. Their visitors have complained to us about the ugly way you treat them and how you belittle their beliefs in addition to the exorbitant fees you charge them. You are acting very selfishly and without showing regard to others. We cannot be silent when we witness and hear about these despicable acts and therefore warn you about mistreating these people and we ask you to extend good

treatment to priests, monks and to Jerusalem's residents of all religious factions and not to overcharge visitors to the River Jordan or the Holy Sepulchre Church. If you obey, it will be in your interest and if not you will be acting against your interests.

Christians and Jews did not forget this stand taken by the Egyptian ruler; they were the only ones who gave him a hero's welcome upon his return to Jerusalem after the uprising started on 13 May 1834, and they also gave him a tremendous reception after defeating rebels at the Battle of Mikhmas (between Jerusalem and Ramallah) on 30 May, [16] demonstrating their love and respect. The Muslim population did not react kindly to this and started a new chain of provocations and rioting. Rebels committed atrocities in the village of Beit Jala where they massacred 33 of its Christian inhabitants and looted houses.[17]

Palestinian rebellions continued in various areas at the instigation of Bab-Al-Ali (the Ottoman government in Constantinople) and other conservative elements in the region who disliked the way Muhammad Ali Pasha and his son Ibrahim cooperated with western countries and the way they copied their customs and habits especially when it came to the army, and they frowned on the policy of establishing equality in treatment between Muslims, Christians and Jews. According to the account left to us by Monk Spirodon, this inclination of Ibrahim Pasha's was an innate part of his character. Writing about the Pasha's return from Jaffa to Jerusalem at the end May 1834, he writes:

> When the Pasha arrived, he dismounted in front of King David's Gate under the scorching heat of the sun. He and his troops did not enter the City but went to the camp that he erected on Mount Zion. After he drank some water, he received dignitaries (Christian Orthodox, Latins, Armenians plus some Jews) who came to welcome the Pasha who saved them from their ordeal. Not a single Muslim was among the welcomers.
>
> When the Pasha asked his visitors about their conditions they praised him and detailed in length the difficulties they had to endure. He encouraged them saying: 'You don't have

to worry anymore, your father has arrived. I came especially for your welfare, but where are the Muslims? Why were there none of them here?' They replied that Muslims were scared of him and that is why they fled. He was astonished and said: 'Why? Who is trying to harm them?'

Monk Spirodon stated that all Jerusalem's Muslims including women and children had left the city before the arrival of the Pasha and headed towards Gethsemane under the burning sun's heat without having any water with them. They were not given any hospitality by the villagers and hence headed for Ramallah, the Christian village that contained 150 Arab Christian Orthodox families who fed them and extended wonderful hospitality to them.[18]

The period of Egyptian rule in Jerusalem provided the monks and monasteries with a golden opportunity to carry out all the restoration work they had not managed to do before, including the quarantine centre in Jaffa that would facilitate the pilgrims' and visitors' journeys to Jerusalem. Ibrahim Pasha contacted Greek and Armenian heads of monasteries stressing the importance of setting up the quarantine centre to prevent the spread of diseases and he suggested siting it in Haifa instead. They replied that it was a good idea but Haifa was too distant and had no Greek monastery. Moreover the road had no rest houses meaning that pilgrims could face mistreatment on the way. For these reasons they sought the establishment of a quarantine centre in Jaffa. When they could not obtain the Pasha's approval they waited until he left for Aleppo, and then petitioned Muhammad Ali Pasha in Egypt. He granted them permission and the Armenians and the Greeks started building their churches in September 1834. The Armenians completed their building on 3 March 1835, ahead of the Greeks since theirs was smaller (30 x 60 metres) while the Greeks completed theirs on 17 March of the same year. The Greek church was a larger structure (60 x 120 metres) and they had to transport stones from Tyre, something they could only do once they had overcome opposition from the Latins and Roman Catholics who built their own quarantine centre in Beirut and wanted to monopolize this important source of income – visitors and pilgrims were, after all, the backbone of commercial activity in the Holy Land, especially in Jerusalem.

The monasteries also obtained permits to repair all damages to buildings that were affected by the earthquake that had occurred on 23 May 1834.

The Latins started repairing their monastery immediately and most repairs, including the foundations, were completed by July 1836.

The Latins also constructed several buildings within the Monastery of Our Lord the Saviour in Jerusalem. The Armenians took the opportunity to greatly enlarge their monastery, annexing a convent to it, and adding a large dome to St James's Church. They added a printing press, a hostel for pilgrims and a large water reservoir in addition to many further improvements inside the courtyards. The Copts also obtained the necessary permits for what they needed to do; they repaired their houses, bought from the Alami family a sesame mill with a large garden all of which came to a total bill of 8,000 girsh (piastres). Once they had removed the mill they constructed a large building covering the total area of the land and designed to accommodate pilgrims coming from Egypt every year. The building cost them 500,000 girsh (piastres).

The clerks who worked in the service of the Pasha, who were Roman Catholics, did not miss out on these opportunities either. They were able to obtain permits to buy several houses near the Coptic monastery on the road to King David's Gate and they built a large monastery and used it to accommodate Roman Catholic priests. A new church was established – one that was to play a significant role in the conflict against the Greek Orthodox, securing a place within the Church of the Holy Sepulchre so that camels could enter the church's yard. They also purchased a large house adjacent to St Ethemios Church at a cost of 50,000 girsh, raised from donations brought from Moscow by the Greek Orthodox Archbishop in Nazareth who was a candidate for the position of Patriarch.[19] It would be a mistake to believe that this activity in construction watered down the secular conflicts that sprang up all the time especially between the Greek Orthodox, Latins and Armenians. The Latins applied for a permit to build a shrine for their sect atop the Mount of Olives, the place of Christ's Ascension, and this too was approved. The Armenians submitted a similar application; the Greek Orthodox reacted by filing a complaint against both sects. As a result, Ibrahim Pasha decided to build a shrine for all sects, but granted the Greek Orthodox a permit to repair the Church of "Half the World" despite the protests of the Latins. He also granted a permit to the Greek Orthodox to repair the Church of Nativity in Bethlehem, in spite of the fact that the Armenians were creating many problems by their repeated violations of the established local rules while the Latins were trying to gain the rights to pass in front of the Holy Tomb while the Greek Orthodox were performing their prayers within the Church of the Holy Sepulchre. This caused a spat which developed into a big fight escalating to a point where weapons were used and in March 1835 the government was obliged to intervene. The Latins pursued their proposals and with the help of their French friends succeeded in persuading Muhammad Ali Pasha to grant them the ownership of the shrine named Christ's Prison and also to give them all of the Church of the Holy Sepulchre with the exception of the part designated for the Greek Orthodox facing the Holy Tomb. They were also granted the ownership of the Notre Dame Church and Bethlehem's Church in addition to the Nativity Cave and the Shepherds' Chapel. The Greek Orthodox community protested strongly and contested all these grants. At the same time the Armenians, through one of their influential dignitaries, Boghas Agha, were able to obtain three Sultanic decrees, approved by Muhammad Ali Pasha, enabling them to rebuild the Church of the Holy Sepulchre, the Mount of Olives Church and the Bethlehem Church which had been badly damaged by the earthquake. They set to work immediately. This was challenged by the monks of the Greek Orthodox monastery who appealed to the nationalistic members of their sect and in the end used force to stop the Armenians from carrying out restoration works.[20] The nationalistic Orthodox sought a peaceful life in this course and yielded all their matters to the hands of the Greek monks who always aimed to control the holy shrines, availing themselves of the benefits provided by the Patriarchate. Hence we note that the rights and properties of the Orthodox citizens were endangered.

The period of Egyptian rule in Palestine, particularly in Jerusalem once the rebellion had been crushed in June 1834, was rather abnormal due to the exceptional circumstances that accompanied it. Ibrahim Pasha employed all possible force available to him to force Jerusalemites to submit to his authority. Hence the four years after 1834 were, for the residents, full of hardship. This suffering was compounded by the spread of cholera in the autumn of 1835 and the disease was to return again in mid-January 1838. A large number of residents and visitors died, including members of the Egyptian army who were billeted in that area.

This succession of events created instability in the region. The lives of the Jerusalemites were further made difficult by the diplomatic efforts and military plans of the British, French and Australians who were acting under the pretext of helping the Ottoman Sultan regain control over his empire. Undoubtedly, they were relieved when they witnessed the Egyptian Army, led by Ibrahim Pasha, withdrawn from the region at the end of 1840, ending their presence of ten long years. We must, however, recognise the big changes that the Egyptian rule made in the region, in particular to the Christian existence in Jerusalem as detailed by historian 'Aref al-'Aref in his book *Al-Mufassal ('An elaboration') on Jerusalem's History*.[21] Al-'Aref notes that the Egyptians:

- Imposed equality between Muslims, Jews and Christians and stopped discrimination against anyone. They also stopped the fees extorted from Christians and Jews under different pretexts.
- Levied *kharaj* tax on Christians in exchange for exempting them from conscription into the army as was the case with Muslims. The word *jizyah* (tax on non-Muslims) was no longer used.
- Foreign merchants were allowed to trade within the country; before they where forbidden to trade except in certain parts and posts.
- The tax which was collected by the Nuseibeh and Joudeh families – the Muslim families who had stood guard at the Holy Sepulchre Church since the days of Saladin – was abolished to encourage visits and pilgrimage.
- The Pasha, in a step to encourage agriculture, abolished the *khums* (literally "fifth") tax which was imposed on farmers' produce. Farmers were encouraged to plant fruit trees and to use modern farming equipment. He also settled a good number of peasants in the plains around Jerusalem and urged them to use it for farming instead of leaving it as pastural land. He also established an agricultural bank to help farmers.
- He encouraged the manufacture of soap in Jerusalem, levying duties on imported soap and putting available stocks of olive oil to good use.
- He fought bribery and put an end to the old habit of presenting gifts to officials.
- He was very active in the field of urban development. He built the Ibrahimiyyeh Complex and constructed a chain of fortresses on the road between Jaffa and Lidda (Lod) to maintain safety for travellers. He paved many roads and made sure that water sources were clean, especially the "Suleiman Pools" which were used to supply Jerusalem with its water needs.
- One of his greatest deeds was when he turned down the request of Sir Moses Montefiore to lease him 50 acres of land and 200 villages for 50

years for a very lucrative sum to be paid in equal annual instalments. His refusal thwarted Sir Moses' plan to bring his Jewish brethren from abroad to settle.

It is believed that Christian Arabs sympathized with the Egyptian presence in the region because of the freedom they felt and the benefits they gained from the increase in commercial activity and the growing numbers of pilgrims and visitors to Jerusalem. The majority of the Christian residents were traders, craftsmen and artisans and stood to benefit from the changes which the Egyptian administration had brought. It is also clear that they could not express their sentiments openly for fear of reprisals by the Muslim majority who opposed Egyptian rule because it confiscated their arms and forcibly conscripted their sons into the army. There was one of the Sultan's Walis (governors) in particular on whom the Muslim community did not look favourably because he forcibly imposed himself as ruler of Bilad al-Sham (Greater Syria) without paying attention to the high degree of respect and esteem that people held for the Caliph of all Muslims in Constantinople.

Notes:

(1) Muhamad Farid, *Tarikh Al-Dawla Al-'Aliya Al-'Othmaniya,* Dar Al-Jeel, Beirut 1977, p.233

(2) 'Aref al-'Aref, *Al-Muffassal Fi Tarikh Al-Quds,* Maktabat Al-Andalus, Jerusalem 1961, p.276

(3) Al-'Aref, *Al-Muffassal Fi Tarikh Al-Quds,* p.276 & 291

(4) Spirodon, "Annals of Palestine 1821-1841" *Magazine of the Eastern Society for Palestine,* Number (18) published in 1938

(5) Asad Rustum, *The Royal Archives of Egypt Declaration of Bilad Al-Sham Documents,* American Press, Beirut, 1940-1952, volume I, p.88

(6) Spirodon, "Annals of Palestine 1821-1841", p.33

(7) Rustum, *The Royal Archives of Egypt Declaration of Bilad Al-Sham Documents*

(8) K.J. 'Asali, ed. Buckhurst Hill, Essex 1989

(9) Latifa Muhamad Salem, *Egyptian Rule in Bilad Al-Sham 1831-1841*, Dar Al-Kitab Al-Jamii', Cairo 1983, pp.153-190

(10) Suleiman Abu Izzedine, *Ibrahim Pasha in Syria*, Al-Matba'ah Al-'Ilmiaya, Beirut, p.139

(11) Spirodon, "Annals of Palestine 1821-1841", p.34

(12) Ibid, p.37

(13) Al-'Aref, *Al-Muffassal Fi Tarikh Al-Quds*, p.397

(14) Spirodon, "Annals of Palestine 1821-1841", p.48

(15) Al-'Aref, *Al-Muffassal Fi Tarikh Al-Quds*, p.280

(16) Ibid, p.283

(17) Ibid, p.283

(18) Spirodon, "Annals of Palestine 1821-1841", p.49

(19) Ibid, p.78

(20) Khalil Ibrahim Qazaqya, *History of the Ecumenical Church of Jerusalem*, Al-Muqtatef press, Cairo 1924, p. (163)

(21) Al-'Aref, *Al-Muffassal Fi Tarikh Al-Quds*, p.288

CHAPTER III

Return of Ottoman Rule (1841)
and the Crimean War (1853-1856)

Without doubt, Muhammad Ali Pasha's campaign to subdue Bilad al-Sham, led by his son Ibrahim Pasha, forced the Ottomans to alter their method of governing. Fundamental changes such as the eradication of bribery and the removal of religious and social barriers all served to deepen the concept of personal freedom as did the introduction of a new method in running military affairs and regulating conscription, training, planning, supply and security checks. The sultans had to review the prevailing conditions within the empire at the time, forcing them to indulge western countries so they could gain their support and assistance and rein in Egyptian expansion. On 3 November 1839 Sultan Abdulmajid, having just assumed power, issued a decree known as the *Al-Khatt Al-Shareef* or *Khatt Hamayon* which signalled a new era of reformation and regulations and which led to the above mentioned change in methodology. The reforms included:

- Organizing the state's administration modernizing the fundamentals of government such as military conscription, the courts and banning expropriations.
- Welfare of their subjects including the abolition of bribery and kickbacks.
- The welfare of non-Muslim subjects and their legal status within the Ottoman State including equal treatment of Muslims, Christians and Jews; also the abolition of fines, stipends, gifts, ill-treatment and exploitation.[1]

Chapter III

The announcement of the *Al-Khatt Al-Shareef* decree and its coincidence with the retreat of the Egyptian army from Bilad al-Sham prompted a strong reaction in Jerusalem, a city which felt it had always deserved a special status among Christians and Jews, whose numbers had increased during the Egyptian rule. One piece of research estimated that Jerusalem's population in 1840 amounted to 11,000 souls, divided as follows: 4,650 Muslims, 3,350 Christians and 3,000 Jews,[2] making Muslims feel like a minority. Nations that competed to gain status among Christians and Jews started buying property and establishing consulates there.

The English were active in this respect, especially since Missionary Nicholson, the first European allowed to live in Jerusalem in 1833, learnt Arabic and Hebrew. He succeeded in establishing a rapport with residents from all sects and offered religious services for Jews and Christians within his mission. He demanded permission to build an English church in Jerusalem. The British government, through its Consul General in Alexandria submitted a request to Muhammad Ali Pasha asking for his permission to allow the London Jewish Society to build a small church along with small buildings to serve the Society's purposes in Jerusalem and also to allow for the appointment of a British consul in Jerusalem. He agreed to the request in full, subject to the approval of the Sultan, the legal ruler. The Sultan, however, was not in a position to approve since Muslim scholars were opposed to granting permits to Christians and Jews to build worshipping places of their own. Moreover, Ottoman law, at the time, did not allow foreigners to own land and properties. In addition, Russia was pressuring the Sultan not to grant a permit for the construction of a Protestant church in Jerusalem.[3]

The Sultan refused to grant the permit to build the church but approved having a British consulate in July 1838. The consulate went on to authorise Nicholson to purchase a plot of land to build a church on, with a part to be used as a cemetery. Nicholson had in previous years leased a house adjoining the Jewish Quarter and used it as his residence. One of its rooms was used for holding daily prayers. He also purchased, in 1833, two plots of land facing King David's citadel near Jaffa Gate, with old dilapidated houses on them. To avoid violating the law he registered these in the names of brokers.

Meanwhile, foreign consulates were allowed to handle all the affairs of their subjects. Britain had already opened its consulate in 1839. Nicholson registered the land in the name of the Society at the consulate confirming that he had paid 750 pounds sterling as its price plus 30 pounds in expenses. The *qadi* (judge) of the religious court who approved this transaction was later relieved of his job for having accepted a bribe.

This success in finding land for the church encouraged the missionary to continue his activity. On 17 December 1839 he started digging the foundations under the supervision of an engineer-surveyor who was brought especially from London, and once they reached a depth of 12 metres in rock they started construction. Stones were brought from quarries in Bethlehem and Anata (north of Jerusalem). Stonemasons from Bethlehem and Ramlah were hired and they worked under the supervision of a craftsman brought from Malta. Nicholson accomplished all these steps in spite of the opposition of the local authorities and the Egyptian administration. Through this he set an example that was followed by other sects who started their construction campaigns within the Holy City.[4]

The French had been similarly active. The French consulate, established in Jerusalem in 1843, extended their protection to Latin and Catholic Christians at the same time as the British consulate was considered the protector of Jews and Protestants. According to the British consul who served in Jerusalem between 1853 and 1856, the first accredited French consul had tried some years before to raise the French flag on the consulate, which led to angry rioting by Muslims who tore it down and dragged it through the streets of the city. The Consul at the time was Paul Emile Botta, a friend of Valerga, the Latin Patriarch, and the son of the Italian historian Carlo Botta who was considered a personal friend of Napoleon Bonaparte. Valerga had met him while he was vice consul in Mosul, Iraq while he headed the congregation there.[5] On 17 July 1848 the Patriarch enthusiastically started his work in Jerusalem[6] aided by a consul who was ever ready to attend all the Church's functions in Jerusalem. He was aided in this policy by the support of the French Foreign Ministry who were always sceptical about the intentions of the Greek Orthodox Patriarchate and the Russian government. The latter also had an eager consul named Bassily who in 1843 became Russian consul in Beirut and also supervised Russian consulates and missions in Aleppo, Latakia, Sidon and Jerusalem.

His instructions were "to pay attention to the religious interests of the Eastern Church which enjoyed the attention of the Imperial Court, and to establish good relations with the heads of other Christian sects, as well as assisting Russian pilgrims". He fulfilled the latter by leasing two monasteries from the Greek Orthodox Church and he started making frequent visits to Jerusalem, where his presence added a special mark to the festivities of the Greek Orthodox and Armenians. These were attended by large numbers of Russian pilgrims, most of whom were ex-members of the military who started bragging by saying "It won't be long before these lands come under the control of the Russian government."[7]

These developments created an atmosphere of unproductive competitiveness for the Christian Arab existence in the Holy Land. Arab influence diminished greatly after the establishment of a number of consulates there – the British in 1838, the Russian in 1843 and the Austrian in 1849 in addition to the Sardinian consulate annexed to the Austrian and the Spanish consulate established in 1854. Conspiracies were knitted daily between the consulates and the patriarchates and churches, none of whom had much Arab influence within them, since the Greeks controlled the Greek Orthodox Patriarchate and its monastery through the Fraternity of the Holy Sepulchre. The Orthodox Patriarch of Jerusalem was until that time residing in Constantinople.

The Arabs among the Latin Church's flock were also a minority, most of them being Orthodox who converted to Catholicism for one reason or another. They were joined by Roman Catholic Arabs motivated by their loyalty to the Vatican in Rome as well as a feeling of importance that they were directed by instructions direct from the Latin Patriarch, backed by France and Austria, for the number of Arab Protestants was also small and most of them converted to Protestantism purely for material gains, especially in education.[8] The situation for the Christian Arabs was very dangerous. The increasing influence of foreign missionaries in the 1840s made the living conditions for the Christian Arabs much worse, especially since their main church, the Orthodox Church, was in a bad state. This worsening in the Church's condition coincided with the expansion of Catholicism which had been active since 1622 when its missionary work had first started, instigated by Jesuit missions. Catholicism was further encouraged at the time of the schism that took place within the Antioch Patriarchate in 1728, when the Roman Catholic Church announced that they would follow the Vatican rather than the Orthodox Church.

Despite the decree signed by the Sultan, forbidding Catholics from preaching among the Orthodox within the Ottoman Empire, as requested by the four Orthodox patriarchs in Constantinople, Alexandria, Antioch and Jerusalem, conversions continued, especially by the Eastern Catholic sects. As a result the number of Latins and Catholics in the Jerusalem area increased from 3,000 in 1840 to 13,000 in 1880 as stated by Derek Hopwood quoting from Russian official sources.[9]

These activities among the different communities and churches in Jerusalem were caused by the tough competition that existed between them and by the desire to occupy distinguished religious, political and military positions. Such aspirations were ultimately to lead to wider conflict: the Crimean War, which started in 1856 under the pretext of religious differences. The root causes of the war, however, were political and military rivalries between the major powers of the time, matters which later spilled over into religious competition. A British consulate was established to counter the French consulate and the Latin patriarchate. This was followed by the establishment of the Anglican archbishopry in Jerusalem to serve all Protestants, something that had been exclusively handled by Jews before. Some English noblemen such as Sir Moses Montefiore, Lord Ashley and Colonel Churchill tried to resume sending Jews to Palestine to carry out agricultural work there.[10] It seems that Churchill was an Anglican zealot; he had connections with Sir Moses Montefiore, who gave cash donations to help poor Jews and to improve the possibilities of work and health services among them,[11] gaining him favour within Jewish and British circles in Jerusalem. An area within the new city was named after him: the Montefiore Quarter.

The procedure of establishing the Anglican archbishopry started when Wilhelm IV, King of Prussia, sent instructions on 8 June 1841 to his emissary at the court of Queen Victoria in London suggesting the rising need to protect British and Prussian subjects and asking him about England's response to granting the national Anglicans in Prussia an equal status with the Church of England in the Holy Land. When the government of England agreed to all the wishes of the Prussian King by having the Church of England establish a bishopry in Jerusalem on Mount Zion encompassing all its institutions and buildings, King Wilhelm immediately donated 15,000 pounds sterling as capital, generating six hundred pounds in interest, payable annually. England donated a similar amount.

Some opposition emerged, mainly from the Oxford Movement, who claimed that the activities of Anglican missionaries led some Jews to convert to Christianity in Jerusalem. In addition, some small Anglican groups were formed which removed any pretext for Latin and Greek Orthodox complaints that some members of their flocks had been converted since the converted Jews did not belong to their Churches. Both Churches were alarmed that the Anglican Church in Palestine might take the lead and responded by trying to exert more spiritual and intellectual effort.[12]

On 5 October, 1841 the decree to establish the Jerusalem bishopry was approved by Parliament in London. It was followed by Queen Victoria's order directed to the Archbishop of Canterbury to appoint Reverend Michael Solomon Alexander, a converted Jew, to be the bishop of the United English and Irish Church in Jerusalem. Meanwhile, Prussia announced its endeavours to ensure that German Evangelists would obtain the same privileges enjoyed by the followers of the Latin and Orthodox Churches within the Ottoman Empire, particularly in Syria and Palestine, since Latin and Orthodox Churches in the Orient relied upon old treaties granting them most of the political rights at the time. In addition the Greek Orthodox Church was under the protection of the Russian Tsar while the Latins were protected by the major Catholic countries. It is for this reason that the Prussian government saw fit to join the Catholic countries in protecting its German Catholic subjects. Indeed, it is worth noting that the Anglican Church was only officially recognized in Turkey very recently. Under these conditions, the Prussian government would now have no obstacles to achieve its objectives which coincided exactly with the feelings of the National Church. We have to note here that the Prussian government, who three decades later became the nucleus of the German Empire, was trying to preserve the rights of its Catholic subjects and also obtain new rights for its National Church, also known as the Lutheran Church. The Lutheran Church was to become a partner with the Church of England in the new bishopry whose head was chosen alternatively by the Crowns of England and Prussia with the Archbishop of Canterbury having the right to veto those nominated by the Prussian (German) crown.[13]

The strong missionary activity that accompanied the inauguration of the Anglican bishopry in 1841 opened the eyes of the Russians who visited Jerusalem in large numbers as pilgrims. The ecclesiastical orientations in Moscow's Patriarchate were always carefully considered by the Russian Imperial Palace. In the same year, the first steps were taken to encourage a Russian presence in Jerusalem when Count Nicholas Brotasov, Secretary-General of the Russian Holy Assembly, recommended dispatching a deacon and two or three monks to Jerusalem. The job was to establish a school within the Orthodox Monastery of the Cross to teach Greek and Russian and also to supervise the distribution of Russian donations and gifts. This recommendation was sent directly to the Tsar who in turn referred them to the Foreign Minister in Moscow, Count Nestlerodeh (a German Protestant), who approved them. The Tsar's official approval came on 3 July 1842 and Archmenderit Porveri Ospinsky was appointed for the job. In September 1843 he visited Constantinople, Syria, Lebanon and Jerusalem where he made various contacts especially with the Greek Orthodox and the Arab Orthodox who, for the first time, felt that Russia cared about them. This appointment confirmed the stiff competition between the representatives of Britain, France and Russia. The instructions he received stressed the importance of gaining the confidence of the Arabs by always talking about the Church as a whole and not about Russia's interests to avoid raising doubts about any political designs behind his mission.[14] Ospinsky was surprised by the reaction of the Orthodox Greeks. During a private conversation he had with the Bishop of Lidda, later Kirellis II, the Greek Orthodox Patriarch of Jerusalem (1845-72), the bishop told him: "Those Arabs are scoundrels who hate us and do damage to our reputation; you can't like us and defend them." Ospinsky replied: "God knows how much I like you but I feel sorry for the Arabs and I am willing to defend them in front of everybody." The bishop said: "They have no faith; they are barbarians and scoundrels." Ospinsky commented: "You should teach them faith; you encouraged their lack of faith; why don't you accept Arab clerics in your ranks? Why don't you help them and also learn Arabic?" The bishop said: "We don't admit Arab clerics within our ranks in order not to lower our clerical standards and we don't learn Arabic because we cannot create new customs." It was a miserable dialogue that showed the Russian emissary the complete lack of trust that existed between the Greeks and the Arabs. It encouraged him to raise the possibilities of Arab development when communicating with the authorities in St Petersburg.[15]

The conflict between the two main components in the largest Christian Church in the Holy Land shows the scandalous neglect of ecclesiastic affairs within the Orthodox Patriarchate of Jerusalem. The Jerusalem Patriarch, who was usually elected and resided in Constantinople, was neither liked nor respected by Orthodox Arabs within the Patriarchate due to his complete disinterest in their affairs. The position ultimately fell vacant for more than two hundred and fifty years.

When Patriarch Kirellis II settled down, he had lots of money at his disposal – huge revenues from the monasteries, lands, properties and endowments that belonged to the Fraternity of the Holy Sepulchre and which was scattered in Serbia, Georgia, the Caucasus, Macedonia, Anatolia, Trakia and elsewhere. This amounted to 30 million girsh per annum, which gave him the nickname of Abu al-Dahab (Father of Gold). He moved his residence to Jerusalem where he opened many elementary schools and upgraded the Jerusalem School. He also established an Arabic printing press in Jerusalem, built several churches and opened the school of theology, known as Al-Musallaba School, within the Monastery of the Cross to discipline the clergy of the Jerusalemite Chair.[16] Here we cannot but note that changes wouldn't have been spontaneous without the changes introduced within the Holy Land by the missionary movements, encouraged also by the recommendations of Ospinsky and by the Russian action that had a great role in the delivery of large amounts of funds to the Orthodox Patriarchate in Jerusalem. These revenues were only affected when Kozmas, the Prince of Romania, took over the 72 monasteries of the Holy Sepulchre during his campaign in 1863 when he captured the properties and endowments of other patriarchates and redirected their revenues to his country's treasury.

Meanwhile, controversies between the Orthodox and the Latin Churches never ceased and each of their protectors had to intervene leading to new conflicts. On 12 October 1847 the Church of Nativity in Bethlehem was visited by the Greek physician of the Orthodox Hospital in Jerusalem, accompanied by two visitors from Greece. They were attacked by the Franciscan friars and, during the skirmish, the Silver Star that was on display in the manger disappeared. The shrine belonged to the Orthodox but the Silver Star had been installed there by the Latins in 1711 when the shrine was under their control, and the Ottoman government had decreed that the Silver Star should stay as a property of the Latins. When it disappeared, the Latins accused the Greek Orthodox of stealing it to have it replaced by a Greek star. Meanwhile, the Greek accused the Latins of taking the star themselves to replace it with a new one since it was old and worn out.

When the complaints reached the Sultan a decree was issued to return the Silver Star to its original place and also to form a committee to look into other rights and financial privileges. The committee released its verdict, which the French Ambassador in Constantinople did not like, so he protested. The Russian Ambassador, meanwhile, had three demands: first, to confirm his legitimate right by issuing another decree; second, to grant the Orthodox Patriarch the right to restore the dome of the Holy Sepulchre Church by the Ottoman government; third, to give Russia the right to protect Christians in Turkey and to co-manage the holy shrines. Turkey agreed to the first two demands and rejected the third since it touched on its dignity and independence. As a result, Russia declared war on Turkey and attacked the provinces on the Danube in October 1853.[18] The outcome of this war did not suit Russian ambitions, for the defeat in 1856 asserted a fundamental change to the Russian relations with the Orthodox East. Russia now had to accept that it was to be treated as equal with the countries that it saw as rivals and who had forced it to sign the Treaty of Paris in 1856 following Russia's defeat in the Crimean War.

These changes were far-reaching and brought misery and shortages of supplies to Jerusalemites. Grain stopped coming from the Crimea because of war operations. Orthodox Christians, especially the Greek Orthodox, had to declare their allegiance to the Sultan, wishing him victory so that they would not be accused of supporting enemies of the State. The Latins and Protestants, on the other hand, had no loyalty issues since the two countries that protected them, France and Britain, were allied with the Ottoman Empire in its war against Russia. The mission, headed by Ospinsky, had to leave Jerusalem in 1853 and Russia could not send another mission until early 1858, headed by Bishop Cyril, who was instructed by the Russian Foreign Ministry to extend all possible assistance to the Orthodox Arabs since Orthodox followers in Syria and Palestine were Arabs. Russia's mission came to be to extend its patronage, to reconcile Arabs and Greeks, and to give assistance to Arabs and not to the pockets of Greek clergymen. The objective of this assistance was to stop Latins from recruiting Arabs to Catholicism.[19]

The great efforts by Latins to preach among Orthodox Arabs and the effort of Protestants to preach among Orthodox Arabs and Jews were met with even greater efforts by the Russians to create better conditions that might facilitate pilgrimage for Russians and improve the living standards of Orthodox Arabs who were the backbone of the Orthodox Patriarchate in Jerusalem. At that time Greek monks were engrossed in their internal conflicts and with disputes with other sects.

All of this activity led to a construction boom in Jerusalem. In 1855, a British tourist named John Gadsby visited Jerusalem. He wrote:

> In reality, Jerusalem has witnessed many changes since 1847; old houses were demolished and palace-like houses were built almost in every street and not only by Christians but also by Muslims. People here are copycats and houses are completed within weeks. All these improvements will make Jerusalem a different city in few years. Land prices have doubled. Despite the extra costs incurred while building St George's and the Protestant Church because of the depth of the foundations yet caretakers can make a tidy profit if they sell those properties tomorrow.[20]

Notes:

(1) Muhamad Farid, p.254, Lutfiyah Salem p.83 and Moshe Ma'oz, *Ottoman Reform in Syria & Palestine (1840-1861)* Clarendon Press, Oxford 1968, p.21

(2) K.J. 'Asali, ed. Buckhurst Hill, Essex 1989

(3) Rafiq Farah, *A History of the Anglican Church in Jerusalem 1841-1991* (Jerusalem) 1995, part 1, p.68

(4) Ibid, p.69

(5) James Finn, *Stirring Times*, 2 volumes Part & Co., London 1878

(6) Allessandro Possetto Il Patriarcato Latino di Gerusaleme, El Cura di Crociata 1938 Mialue

(7) Derek Hopwood, *The Russian Presence in Syria and Palestine, 1843 – 1914: Church and Politics in the Near East* (Clarendon Press, Oxford, 1969)

(8) Ibid

(9) Ibid, p.31

(10) Finn, *Stirring Times*, p.39

(11) Farah, *A History of the Anglican Church in Jerusalem 1841-1991*, p.75

(13) Ibid, p.89

(14) Hopwood, *The Russian Presence in Syria and Palestine, 1843 – 1914: Church and Politics in the Near East*, p.36

(15) Ibid, p.38

(16) Ibid, p.44

Shehada Khoury and Nichola Khoury: (in Arabic) *Khulasat Tareekh Kanisat Jerusalem Al- Urthudoxiyyah*: (Jerusalem Printing Press, 1925)

(18) Finn, *Stirring Times*, p.73

(19) Hopwood, *The Russian Presence in Syria and Palestine, 1843 – 1914: Church and Politics in the Near East*, p.47

(20) John Gadsby, *My Wanderings: Being Travels in the East (between 1846 and 1860)*, 2 vols. (Gadsby, London, 1855-1860), vol. 2, p.491

CHAPTER IV

General Conditions in Jerusalem
During the mid-19th Century

T he Crimean War ended with the Paris Convention on 25 February, 1856 signed by France, Britain, Russia, Sardinia and the Ottoman Empire, with Austria and Prussia participating. The Paris Convention confirmed that, ultimately, all these countries simply wanted to accept the status quo. Article nine read as follows:

> The Sultan of the Ottoman State, in his endeavours to improve the life of his subjects, has issued a decree aiming to better their conditions irrespective of their religions. He wants to show goodwill towards Christians residing in his domain. To show his good intentions, he wants the signing countries to see the decree that he signed in good faith and to see the benefits that this decree gives them. But it is also implicitly understood by this decree that signing countries should in no way seek, singly or collectively, to do any harm to the Sultan or to any part of his domain or to intervene in the Sultan's managing the internal affairs of his country. [1]

The Greek monks considered 1856 as the year when the status quo in the Holy Land was confirmed, especially once the Sultan had issued his *Khatt Hamayon* recognizing the rights of his non-Muslim subjects and equal treatment for all, regardless of faith. From that point onwards Christians were conscripted into the army exactly like Muslims.[2]

The decree aimed at weakening Russia's demand to protect the rights of its Orthodox subjects within the Ottoman Sultanate at a time when all other countries, collectively, refused any right to interfere in the internal affairs of the Sultanate.[3]

The main reason to protect the status quo was that the holy places had been, for thirteen centuries, under non-Christian rule, when privileges and rights for sects and churches could only be obtained by gifts and bribery or by diplomatic pressure or through other means. The holy places in question are: the Church of the Holy Sepulchre and its courtyard, the Church of Virgin Mary in Gethsemane, the Church of the Ascension on the Mount of Olives in Jerusalem and the Sultan Monastery atop the Church of the Holy Sepulchre.

When disputes about rights within churches were renewed in the early 19th century, the authorities always referred to the Status Quo Policy which was approved by the treaties of Paris, Vienna and Berlin and by the Sultan's decrees of 1868 and 1869, and which became standard policy followed later by the British, Jordanians and the Israelis from 1918 until now. The sects that have rights to these holy shrines are: the Greek Orthodox, Franciscan Latins, Armenian Orthodox, Copts and the Assyrian Orthodox only.[4]

The total area of the Old City in Jerusalem is 927 dunums (a dunum is 1,000 square metres) distributed among various parties as follows:[5]

Table 4.1
Total areas owned by the three religions and government services locations in Jerusalem (in dunums):

Christian Properties	420
Muslim Properties	405
Jewish Properties	40
Government Servia locations areas	62
Total	927

Christians within the city are divided into Eastern and Western Churches following different leaderships.

The Eastern Churches are divided into:
• Greek Orthodox Patriarchate
• Armenian Orthodox Patriarchate
• Coptic Bishopry
• Assyrian Orthodox Bishopry/Monastery
• Russian Church and the Church of Kurj (Georgia)

The Western Churches are divided into:
• Latin Patriarchate
• Roman Catholic Diocese
• Armenian Catholic Diocese
• Assyrian Catholic Diocese
• Assembly of Evangelics – Arab Bishopry
• German Missions

EASTERN CHURCHES

Greek Orthodox Church
Patriarchs in this period were Polikarius (1808-1827), Athanasios V (1827-1845) and Kirellis II (1845-1872). It was Kirellis II who was responsible for returning the seat of the Patriarchate to Jerusalem after it was abandoned by previous Orthodox Patriarchs for nearly two centuries.

During his tenure, Patriarch Kirellis purchased the houses adjoining Damascus Gate, known as the Khdeir houses from the Khalidi family. Once they had been repaired, the complex was used to house native Orthodox Christians and called Spirodon Monastery. He also built the arcade that connects the central monastery with the Patriarchate.

When Grand Duke Constantine, brother of the Russian Tsar Alexander, paid an official visit to Jerusalem on 30 April, the Patriarch organized a magnificent welcoming reception for him, which prompted him to make generous gestures towards charity work and to encourage Russian presence in the Holy Land. Here we have to remember that most of the properties belonging to the Patriarchate were not in Jerusalem nor even in the Holy

49

Land but were in Serbia and other Romanian regions, and we note that the endowments confiscated on 13 November 1862 were within lands Russia annexed to its territories in 1812 after the Treaty of Bucharest.[6] The loss of these properties led the Fraternity of the Holy Land to urge nationals to bequeath lands to the Patriarchate and also to buy lands in Jerusalem's suburbs and in other areas in Palestine since their properties there had previously been restricted to sites within the Old City.

There are conflicting stories about the reasons that compelled Patriarch Kirellis II to move his residence from Constantinople to Jerusalem. There were probably many reasons that led him to take this momentous decision. The presence of the Patriarchate in Jerusalem, away from Constantinople, confirmed his independence, enabling him to act without going back to the Patriarch of Constantinople. In addition, he had to face the important developments that resulted from the establishment of the Anglican Bishopry in Jerusalem and the growth of Latin influence that proved itself by the re-establishment of the Latin Patriarchate. Some believe that the struggle over the Holy Shrines which existed between the Greek Orthodox from one side and the Latins and Armenians from the other made the Greek presence in Jerusalem more effective, because the monks of the Fraternity of the Holy Sepulchre sensed that the leverage they enjoyed over many Christian matters by virtue of their relation with the Sultan and the Government (via the Al-Fanar Patriarchate in Constantinople) would have been threatened.

There is, however, an Orthodox Arab point of view mentioned in the book *A Historical Glimpse at the Greek Fraternity of the Holy Sepulchre*, by Bishop Raphael Hawawini. It says:

> When the Jerusalem Patriarchate's seat was filled by Kirellis, the bishop of Lidda in 1845, he soon moved his Patriarchal base from Constantinople to Jerusalem, driven not by his wish to serve his local flock, but by his desire to be free from the ambitions of Al-Fanar Clerics, i.e. the Patriarchate of Constantinople. When he reached Jerusalem, however, and witnessed the great success achieved by the Latins and noted how they established schools and printing presses to enlighten the inhabitants, he became worried about the Fraternity of the Holy Sepulchre and the possibility of its disintegration, for its members were drowning in ignorance and stupidity and were

only concerned in collecting money and spending lavishly. He wanted to correct that so he built them a theology school within the Kurj Monastery. They allowed the sons of some Orthodox Arabs to enrol as students but they were not given the same treatment as the Orthodox Greeks' sons who were allowed to live in the school for the duration of the six academic years it took to graduate.[7]

In reality, the Patriarch's move to Jerusalem and the elections held there were an operation of independence for the Jerusalem Church, freeing it from the traditional subordination to the Patriarchate of Constantinople. This was confirmed when a struggle erupted between the Church of Bulgaria and the Greek Church in general (discussed in Chapter V).

The Greek Patriarchate is the largest Church when it comes to the number of its subjects, properties and endowments. In a later chapter we have a list published by the Greek monks stressing the significance and size of these endowments which, unfortunately, were later to be targeted by the Israeli authorities. A large part of the endowments were sold with another large part leased for periods up to 99 years. This led to a dispute between Greek monks who controlled the Patriarchate, headed by Patriarch Theodorus, and Orthodox Arabs who tried to warn the authorities and all Arabs of the great risks that would result from Arabs losing control over these endowments – especially since they are used by the Israeli authorities as settlement sites as part of the operation to establish the Israeli state as a "fact on the ground". This is especially true of the first *qibla* in the Old City, the third holiest place for Muslims, and the mother of all churches for all Christians.

Armenian Orthodox Patriarchate

We noted earlier, that the Armenian Orthodox were always competing with the Greek Orthodox over the right to control certain holy shrines. It is certain that the increased number of Armenian pilgrims to Jerusalem since the start of the 19th century strengthened their position in Jerusalem. Their presence there dates back to the 12th century, when they had three churches on the Mount of Olives and a fourth near Damascus Gate. Apparently their churches increased in number after the 16th century. Olya Jalabi, the Turkish explorer who visited the city in 1670, mentioned that he saw two Armenian churches.[8]

Armenian properties in Jerusalem are numerous and occupy large areas; they are mentioned in detail by 'Aref Al-'Aref in his book *Christianity in Jerusalem*.[9] It is important to note that the Monastery of Mar Ya'qoub that occupies a huge area of land and includes the Patriarchate, where the Patriarch resides, and the theology school, the printing press and two libraries, with one having 3,700 manuscripts and the other 35,000 printed volumes, was always subject to dispute between the Armenians and the Roman Orthodox who both laid claim to ownership. The dispute was only settled in 1735 by the *Mahkama Shar'iyyeh* (religious court) where the judge ruled in favour of the Armenians, having heard the testimonies of the heads of the Coptic, Abyssinian and Assyrian sects as well as testimonies of Muslim scholars, imams, leaders and also merchants and feudal lords in Jerusalem at the time. It is clear from the records of that court that after 1761 the Armenian Monastery purchased two houses from Abdallah Effendi, the son of the chief of Al-Ashraaf in Jerusalem (Husseini family), and endowed them to benefit poor Armenian priests residing at Mar Ya'qoub Monastery in Jerusalem.

We note here that the Armenian Patriarch in Jerusalem reported to the Armenian authorities in Constantinople until 1917. This is similar to the structure within the Roman Orthodox Patriarchate until 1845 when Kirellis moved his headquarters to Jerusalem ridding himself of control by the Orthodox Patriarch of Constantinople. In both cases, the presence of Jerusalem's Patriarchs in Constantinople provided Patriarchs of Constantinople with many privileges which they used as tools to impose their control over local churches within the States of the Ottoman Empire.

The Coptic Bishopry

Coptic ties to Jerusalem go back to the early Christian era due to the strong relationship with the Holy Land dating from when the Holy Family visited Egypt. Their pilgrimage visits stopped, however, during the Crusader period. When Saladin came, they were revitalized. Saladin sought to reward them for their loyalty so he returned to them most of the properties, churches and monasteries which they had owned before his rule. They enjoyed a further age of government support some seven hundred years later when the armies of Muhammad Ali Pasha, led by his son Ibrahim Pasha, overran Bilad al-Sham in 1831. The number of Copts increased during this period, rising from a base that had dropped very low according to Ottoman archives from when they ruled the area in the early 16th century. Al-'Aref mentions that in the early 20th century the Copts numbered around 1,300, a number which was to increase by the end of the British Mandate, reaching 10,000 in 1948, with the number of Coptic pilgrims reaching more than 3,000 annually.[10]

The Assyrian Orthodox Bishopry

Al-'Aref mentions that the number of Assyrians residing in Jerusalem towards the end of the British Mandate (1945) was around 2,000. They had lived in Jerusalem since the first century AD and followed the Patriarchate of Antioch and the Middle East for the Assyrian Orthodox. In Jerusalem their matters were managed by the Jerusalem Orthodox Assyrian Bishop until the mid 20th century. In 2000 they were headed by the deputy Patriarch of the Assyrian Orthodox in Jerusalem based in Mar Marcus Monastery in the Al-Sharq district between the Armenians and the Jewish districts. It contains the upper room where Jesus had the Last Supper with his disciples at the dawn of Christianity. The monastery was enlarged and restored in 1855. The Assyrian Orthodox also have a small chapel within the Holy Sepulchre behind the Copts' Church west of the Holy Tomb, as well as an altar within Our Lady Mary's Church in Gethsemane. They were able to purchase property in the area north-east of Al-Maskobiyya in 1872, and also owned Dair Al-Adas, thought to be the place where St Peter was incarcerated.

It is clear that oscillating conditions and the shortage in numbers of Assyrians in the Holy Land have weakened their position. In a pamphlet issued in 2000 by the Patriarchate, headed by Patriarch Ignatius Zakka I Iwaz, Patriarch of Antioch and the Middle East and the head of the Orthodox Assyrian Church worldwide, we find a modern analysis of these condition when he says: "The tough political circumstances that this area witnessed during the last 400 years have greatly weakened the Assyrian Church; it lost lots of its properties and saw its sons emigrating to distant locations." Despite that, they are still in the Holy Land, proud that they have important rights in the Holy shrines and also some humble yet historically significant properties. One of their endowments in the Holy City is Mar Marcus Monastery, the oldest monastery in Jerusalem, plus the Church of Our Lady Mary believed to be on the site where Jesus had the Last Supper. They also have other properties around the monastery: Mar

Bahnam's Church behind Mar Marcus Monastery plus a school, some houses occupied by Assyrians and the Assyrian Club.

The Assyrian Orthodox Patriarchate is among the five churches that have rights in the Holy Sepulchre Church, The Church of Nativity, Church of Virgin Mary and the Church of Ascension on the Mount of Olives[11] as dedicated by the "Status Quo".

The Abyssinian Bishopry

From the start, the number of Abyssinians in Jerusalem was small. The Abyssinian Church was considered an offshoot of the Coptic Church. The head of their monastery in Jerusalem used, in ancient times, to be inducted by the Coptic Patriarch in Egypt. In spite of that, there were continuous disputes between Abyssinians, Copts and Armenians during the 19th century, always about properties and places of worship. The reason for the chronic dispute is made clear when reading al-'Aref's book *Christianity in Jerusalem*[12] when he writes: "The Armenians continued to provide the Abyssinians daily with two boxes of soap and 75 loaves of bread for 40 girsh (10 francs) the same way they did for the last 160 years when they nearly perished by hunger." So the Armenians volunteered to supply them with these provisions in return for Abyssinians relinquishing their rights in the Holy Sepulchre Church.

Dair Al-Sultan monastery, adjacent to the Holy Sepulchre Church, is considered to be the Abyssinians' headquarters in Jerusalem. It is the place where the Bishop of the Orthodox Abyssinians resides. This monastery caused conflict with the Copts who claimed they owned it, and that they allowed Abyssinians to use it because they were poor. It seems that the poverty of Abyssinians living in Jerusalem and their small number made them the target of the greed of neighbouring Copts and Armenians, for their numbers diminished until they dropped as low as about 20 in 1823. In 1851 they had a major disagreement with the Copts about the key to Dair Al-Sultan, where they lived. The court ruled that the Copts should keep the key thus enabling them to control the movement of the Abyssinian monks and other members of the flock who lived there. Before that they were subjected to a different type of ordeal, during Egyptian rule, when their library, containing a large number of books and manuscripts, was burnt at the orders of Ibrahim Pasha. The Abyssinians were ordered to hand the keys of the Chapel within Dair Al-Sultan to the Copts.

The Abyssinians' affairs, however, did not continue to be all bad, for at the end of the 19th century they benefited from a good and honest head of the Church, Father Jiryes, who was able to convey their complaints to Nijashi John, the King of Abyssinia, who started sending funds to Jerusalem, sufficient to meet the needs of Abyssinians there. In this way they were able to hold onto some of their properties. Father Jiryes was also able to purchase land outside Jerusalem's Walls where he built a monastery and a beautiful church.

Later, the family of Emperor Menlik bought three large houses that were endowed to benefit Dair Al-Sultan and to cover the expenses of the monks there. Emperor Menlik himself was personally interested and he deposited in their name 200,000 Austrian thaler (worth 750,000 French francs at the time) with Crédit Lyonnais, the French bank, in 1905. Their conditions changed, they regained their status and became more independent in carrying on their day-to-day affairs.[13]

The Russian Church and the Church of Kurj (Georgia)
The end of the Crimean War in 1856 was a turning point in Russian relations with the Orthodox East. It was clear that Russia's dream to occupy a special place in the Ottoman Empire was no longer possible. Russia had to deal with its competitors on an equal footing. As a result, talk started within Russian circles concerning the steps to be taken with regards to the situation in Syria. The most concerned about this were the Tsar, the Archbishop of St Petersburg (who was the dean of Orthodox Priests at the Tsar's Court), Count Tolstoy, the minister of the Holy Synod, and Count Gorshakov, the foreign minister. Sending a new mission to Jerusalem was discussed. After deliberations, the Tsar approved the appointment of Bishop Policarp in April 1857 thus excluding Ospinski who was an expert on the Holy Land. Policarp resigned shortly thereafter, however, which made the Holy Synod exclude Ospinski for the second time and appoint Archmenderit Cyril once they had secured the Tsar's hesitant approval. He was promoted to the post of Bishop of Miltopol before leaving Russia to assume his new position in Jerusalem.

When looking closely at the Russian Foreign Ministry's objectives when it approved sending the mission to Syria and the Holy Land we see the extent to which the plan was connected to the objectives of Russian Policy.

The Foreign Ministry's decisions stipulated that:

> First, our existence in the East should not be political but
> through the Church because the Turks and the Europeans who
> have Patriarchs and Bishops in the Holy City cannot object.
> Jerusalem is the centre of the World and our main rule should
> be there. Second, we must support and assist the Orthodox
> Arabs for up until now we have looked at the Church in
> Palestine and Syria from a Greek perspective, and the Greek
> monks were the sole recipients of all Russian aid. That was in
> spite of the fact that the Orthodox faithful in Antioch and
> Jerusalem and to a lesser extent in Alexandria were all Arabs
> who did not receive any part of that aid. We also should build
> schools and print Arabic books in Jerusalem. Third, we should
> look after the moral supervision of the increasing numbers of
> Russian pilgrims during their visit to Palestine. Fourth, we
> should open a Russian printing press in Jerusalem.[14]

A new movement started, headed by the Grand Duke Constantine
Nicholavich (1827-1892), the second son of Tsar Nicholas I, who was then
interested in establishing a shipping company that would be able to
transport large numbers of Russian pilgrims to the Holy Land, thus
lessening dependence on Austrian and Italian ships. Based on detailed
reports about this project, the Tsar gave his orders in March 1858 to
establish the Palestine Committee and appointed Cyril Nomov as its head,
provided that Ospinsky should accompany him during his first visit. The
group who established this committee was aiming to rid Russian pilgrims
of Greek exploitation during their time in the Holy Land. They also decided
to pay the salaries of Arab clergymen in Palestine. This decision was never
executed and remained on paper only.[15] Bishop Cyril reached Palestine
early in1858 and left Jaffa for Jerusalem in a large convoy that included the
Russian consul general in Beirut, Greek and Armenian monks and a large
gathering of Russian pilgrims. At the head of the convoy, when it left
Ramlah, was a team of honour guards sent by the governor of Jerusalem. It
consisted of one Agha and ten cavalrymen. The arrival in Jerusalem was a
victorious demonstration that gave the Greeks the impression that this
success would be at their expense, since it would decrease their revenues

received from Russian churches and Russian pilgrims. Such worries were to be proven to be justified for from the start of 1859 the Russian funds were transferred to the Palestine Committee which was able, between 1859 and 1864, to collect one million roubles from its fund-raising campaign throughout Russia.

The Committee collected 300,000 roubles from churches within Russia, 200,000 roubles from societies and individuals and 500,000 roubles from the Tsar and the Russian government. These funds were used to purchase lands negotiated by the Grand Duke Constantine during his state visit to the Holy Land. The land included the large Midan lot north of Jerusalem which was used for the military parades of the city's Turkish garrison and was also used by the inhabitants as a recreational park. Also purchased were four land lots near the city's walls as well as a small lot within the walls and a large lot on the Mount of Olives. The Grand Duke was very enthusiastic about the whole project and on his return home he oversaw the preparation of the drawing plans for the buildings to be constructed in Palestine. Work started, but it was slow, and the only completed parts of the grand project by 1863 were the mission's house and the hospital. During work on the project, men resided at the women's hostel and the Cathedral for some years. On completion of the big project, named Al-Maskobiyya by the city's residents, Russia was in a position to fulfil its objectives and take the lead, divesting itself of the relation with Greece, and also providing better services to Arabs and to the subjects of other Slavic countries.[16] Consequently, Russian pilgrims were allowed to use these houses without any fees or charges.[17] In this period Russia established its first consular presence in Jerusalem, opened in 1858 initially as consular representative for the shipping company and subsequently in 1863 as the base for the consulate. Al-Maskobiyya became a symbol of Russia's stature and strength.

The Kurj Church, which is the Arabic term given to the Church of Georgia (South Caucasus), was of great significance over the ages. Narratives mention that Dair Al-Musallaba originally belonged to the Kurj and was built in AD 342 during King Mariam's visit to Jerusalem. Another story, from a Kurj document at the library of the Roman Orthodox Monastery in Jerusalem, mentions that the Dair (monastery) was built by the Kurj in 1038 and later became the property of the Roman Orthodox Monastery, left unused until it served as the headquarters of the school of theology established by the Orthodox Church in 1855.[18]

Another story says that Mar (Saint) Jacob Monastery, or the Grand Armenian Orthodox Monastery, belonged originally to the Kurj and then to the Greeks who later leased it to the Armenians,[19] who later became the owners. These stories confirm the historical facts that Kurj (Georgia) suffered greatly from Persian attacks during the 17th century, leading to cessation of aid sent to monasteries in Palestine – something which burdened Kurj monks with heavy debts and left them no choice but to return to their country. After that, the Greek Orthodox settled the debts and took over the Kurj properties and endowments.[20]

WESTERN CHURCHES

Latin Patriarchate

The first patriarch for the Holy City was Monsignor Giuseppe Valerga who started preparations for establishing the Latin Patriarchate in Jerusalem during January 1848. During his leadership, which lasted until 1872, the Patriarchate accomplished a great deal for the Latin Church through his pastoral work and through the setting up of centres in Palestine and Transjordan. Here we have to mention that the Latins' relations with the Ottoman State was strengthened in 1535 when a treaty was signed with the French State whereby the rights of Latins in Jerusalem were confirmed, granting them the rights of visiting and staying. In 1740 another treaty was signed granting the Latins basic rights in the holy sites such as the right of movement and the right to establish churches and monasteries. France was considered, according to this treaty, as "Protector of Christianity in the Near East."[21] That period was, probably, the time when the Latin Church became the main competitor to the Orthodox Church for everything that concerned the holy sites in Palestine.

When he arrived in Jerusalem in 1848, having been appointed by Pope Pius IX, Patriarch Valerga discovered that his flock did not exceed 4,000 in number with 900 of them living in Jerusalem. He was also astonished to see that his parish was divided, one faction supporting the Pope and his emissary, the new Patriarch, while the other faction supported the Franciscan monks, the guards of the holy shrines who were entrusted by Pope Gregory IX to serve and protect the Holy Sepulchre Church in 1236. To strengthen his position, the new Patriarch encouraged European monks to come to the

Holy Land[22] which they did and their numbers increased. This enabled the Patriarch to strengthen his position and provide better pastoral services to the Latin congregations in the areas of Nazareth, Jerusalem, Bethlehem, Lidda and Ramlah in Palestine, and the regions of Al-Hosn, Ajloun and Al-Salt in Transjordan.[23]

The Latins' endowments in Jerusalem were many. There is more on this in a later chapter showing a list of the properties published by the Latin Patriarchate in 1984. We also have to mention that the Latins are one of the sects that have rights laid down in the Status Quo Policy that followed the Crimean War. Aside from their rights in the Holy Sepulchre Church, the Virgin Mary's Church in Gethsemane and the Church of Ascension on the Mount of Olives, they also had Dair Al-Mukhalles (the Monastery of the Saviour) also known as the Latins' Monastery within Harat Al-Nasara (the Christian Quarter) which they purchased in 1559.[24] It has a library, a church, an orphanage, a pharmacy, a printing press, a bakery, a mill and several workshops in addition to several water reservoirs that were completely essential for life in Jerusalem. They also owned the hostel designate to receive pilgrims at the New Gate and the Patriarchate building adjoining it, plus the Church of Gethsemane which is of great beauty, built in 1924 from Latins' donations around the world. It is built on the site where, it is said, Christ was captured by the Jewish Chief Rabbi and the Roman governor, having been betrayed by Judas Iscariot. The Latin Church also owned several monasteries built throughout the years by different monastic orders, plus the Austrian Hospice, built in 1756, which was to become the only hospital within the city walls after the 1948 War.

Despite the difficulties Patriarch Valerga faced when he assumed office, he is credited with establishing the school of technology that opened its doors before the end of 1852 in a building near his house after he acquired it from the organization responsible for preserving holy places at the end of 1851. It is worthy of note that an atmosphere of openness and freedom ruled in this school, completely the opposite to the atmosphere of oppression and racism imposed by the Greek monks in the Orthodox education system. A list of names of students who enrolled at the school between 1852 and 1856 shows that most were Arabs: Antoun Dikha, Simon Isaac, Antoun Murqus and Antoun Qaisar from Jerusalem; Yousef Tannous, Hanna Sarina and Antoun Rizq from Nazareth; Hanna Merta from Biet Jala. In addition there were five youths from Cyprus among whom were Arabs such as Emile

Zakharia and Arabists like Charles Catoni and Maronites like Antoun Bartella.[25]

That period of the Latins' history in Jerusalem was rife with educational and social activity. In addition, Franciscan and Carmelite monks were in the Holy Land for more than 200 years. The Nuns of St Joseph started their activities in 1948; the Sisters of Zion in 1856; the Carmelite Nuns in 1853; the Monks of Zion in 1873; the Frères Monks in 1876; the White Fathers in 1878; the Monks of St Joseph and the Fathers of the Sacred Cover in 1879.[26]

The Roman Catholic Diocese

The diocese was established in Jerusalem in 1848 and is located within the Maronite Quarter. It includes The Church of the Virgin's Annunciation as well as a hostel for visitors, and serves as the residence of the Patriarch in Jerusalem. 'Aref Al-'Aref mentions that Roman Catholics (known also as Melkites) in Jerusalem numbered 800 in 1945 while their numbers in the whole of Palestine totalled 30,000.[27] Their other properties in Jerusalem were few, however, but included the House of St Veronica located at the 6th stage of the Via Dolorosa which they bought for 3,000 French gold Napoleons, perhaps in 1879, from Abdul Rahman Hadduta al-Alam after which they built a church on the site once they had obtained a Sultan's decree in 1894. They also own St Anne's Church situated between Bab Hutta and the Gate of Our Lady Mary north of Al-Haram which is the place, according to narratives, of the house of Joachim and Anne (Hannah), parents of Virgin Mary.

The Society of White Fathers monks who came to Jerusalem in 1878 had previously bought a large lot of land and built a residence and a school which were visited by the Roman Catholic Patriarch in 1880. He requested that they turn it into a clerical college for Roman Catholics in the Holy Land. Once they had cleared this with Pope Leo XIII it was turned into a college for Roman Catholics. Over the years a large number of bishops and Arab clerics graduated from this college. During 1947, due to the events in Palestine, it was moved to Homs in Syria.[28]

The Armenian Catholic Diocese

This group seceded from the Armenian Orthodox Church after the schism between the Roman Orthodox and the Roman Catholics in the early 18th century. They established a presence in Jerusalem by setting up a house for the Patriarchate and a church named The Pains of the Virgin in 1886 at Al-Wad Quarter between the third and fourth stages of the Via Dolorosa. They were authorised in this by an order from Constantinople to the Governor of Jerusalem, with the conditions that they leave five metres to be a road between their house and the Qadiri and Naqshbandi Zawiyas which are 60 metres from Al-Haram, and that the area of the church should not exceed 25.5 metres in length, 10.5 metres in width and 13 metres in height. They were allowed to build 22 rooms for visitors, and a suitable stable to meet the deputy Patriarch's need even though the number of Armenian Catholics at the time did not exceed 22 persons (four families).[29]

The Assyrian Catholic Diocese

This diocese branched out from the Assyrian Orthodox Church. In 1872 they became stronger when they followed the faith of the Roman Latin Church in Rome. They established for themselves an independent leadership headed by a Patriarch that was followed by dioceses in Syria, Lebanon, Iraq, Egypt, Palestine and Jordan. Their numbers in 1945 were not more than 400 persons,[30] headed by the deputy Patriarch in the Holy City. Most of the endowments and properties of the Assyrian Catholics are relatively new. The monastery and the church lie between the Church of Notre Dame and Damascus Gate, and were built in 1901. They also own Mar Mubarak Monastery (also called St Benedictus Monastery) which lies on top of a hill in Silwan Village and was built in 1903 on a plot of land purchased from the people of Silwan three years earlier. The monastery has a clerical school run by Benedectine monks.[31] The diocese in Jerusalem studied all decrees and orders in the archives of the Islamic Sharia Court, and concluded that they had been a prestigious sect during the rule of the Mamluks in the 15th century.

The Maronite Diocese

The presence of Maronites in Jerusalem is old but seems to have weakened after the Crusaders' Wars. Their presence, however, was revitalized when Bishop Elias Al-Howayyik, sent by the Patriarch of the Maronites in Lebanon in 1893, attended a sacrificial mass headed by Cardinal Larenget. Two years later he visited Jerusalem and purchased a plot of land from the German consul on which he built a church and a building for the Maronite

Patriarchate, known as the Maronite Batrakhanah. Here he supervised the matters of the Maronites who numbered fewer than 500 in 1948[32] and whose numbers were to decline steadily until there were as few as 60 by1950.

The Protestant Diocese

The importance of this diocese is that it was connected to Great Britain – the superpower of the 19th century. Although it started as a result of joint cooperation with Prussia, Britain had the larger role in establishing and strengthening the diocese. Its strength was out of proportion with the number of Christians that became members of its Anglican and Lutheran churches. In the third chapter we discussed how missionary activities started, and how the Sultan turned down a petition to build a Protestant church in Jerusalem but approved building a British consulate in July 1838. Matters developed after 1839 when the British Parliament issued an ordinance, named Ordinance of the Diocese of Jerusalem, approving the establishment of the church. The appointed bishop for this diocese was Michael Solomon Alexander, a former Jew who had been baptised in Plymouth Church in June 1825.[33]

Bishop Alexander reached Jerusalem via Beirut, Jaffa and Ramlah where he was amazed by the Arab hospitality he received at the house of Murqos Abboud, the US consul. Despite the support he received from the British Consular Service, he faced resistance from the French and from the churches under French protection, especially the Jesuits. He also met with resistance from the Jews, specifically those who were the subject of his main mission to convert them to Christianity. As for the Roman Orthodox, despite good relations with them from the time he was their guest for some months at Dair Al-Musallaba, opening the new diocese and increasing Protestant missionary activity caused Patriarch Kirellis to return from Constantinople and reside permanently at the Orthodox Patriarchate in the Holy City. Meanwhile, Wilhelm IV, the King of Prussia, who was following the news about the diocese with interest, appointed a Prussian consul in Jerusalem in 1843, the same year that France appointed its consul in the Holy City. It is worth noting that Bishop Alexander, who died in 1845, succeeded in converting 39 Jews to Christianity, making the number of Protestants in Jerusalem that year about 60 persons including 21 missionaries.[34]

Queen Victoria appointed Bishop Alexander, as per the rotation agreement signed by Britain and Prussia when establishing the diocese.

Hence, the King of Prussia appointed, as his successor, Bishop Samuel Gobath who arrived in Jerusalem on 30 December 1846. He took a different path than his predecessor, giving Jews little attention and directing his efforts instead towards Eastern Christianity by opening schools for Christian Arabs. The first school he opened was the Bishopric Boarding School for boys later known as Bishop Gobath School. He then opened the School of Zion. In 1847 he opened a day school for the boys of Jerusalem. He also strengthened his ties with the Christian Missionary Society (CMS)[35] who were later very active in clerical and social services especially in education. It established branches for itself in Jerusalem, Nazareth, Haifa, Jaffa and Nablus. The number of Protestant schools in the country by 1882, three years after the death of Bishop Gobath, had reached 35 schools for boys and girls with a total of 1,635 students.[36] This was a clear indication of the importance given to this region by Britain before it the situation developed and the region became of the utmost importance following the British Occupation of Egypt later that year.

It seems that the bishop's activities provoked various factions in Jerusalem and led to protests. As a result the British Consul issued an order preventing the bishop from leaving Jerusalem. Upon hearing about this, the Foreign Minister wrote to the Consul threatening to remove him from his position.[37] With this support Bishop Gobath was able to actively continue his work until he died in 1879.

The Assembly of the Arab Diocese for the Evangelical Sect

The Christian Missionary Society (CMS) was established in Palestine and Transjordan at the end of the 18th century in London. Its objective was to discuss all ecclesiastical issues including the issue of the missionaries. During the tenure of Bishop Gobath special attention was focused on Christian Arabs within the Eastern Churches. This task was entrusted to the CMS who in turn gave it to the National Church whose leadership was given to a national priest, a citizen of the land. Credit in this transformation goes to the priest John Fenn who stuck to the Church's tenet of giving laymen an important role, so that control of managing the Church and its project was left in the hands of bishops and ordained priests. This was based on the three main rules of the national churches: financial independence, self-rule and self-expansion. The Assembly's mission was restricted to encouraging national churches to bear their own responsibilities. Once that had been achieved, the Assembly could withdraw from the field of national churches.[38] This was an important tenet that the Latin Church could not really absorb until 1888 when Patriarch Michel Sabah was installed as Patriarch of the Latins. The Orthodox Patriarchate was still suffering badly from Greeks controlling the main positions, without being aware of the importance of having nationals sharing in managing and servicing their own churches. When the Church became strong, it started building St Paul's Church outside the City Walls in the street where the Queen of Abyssinia Street branches from it, near Al-Mascob Land. The church was inaugurated in 1874. It was endowed by the Protestant Awdah Azzam, originally from Nazareth, who endowed all his properties which were located inside Damascus Gate, opposite Al-Khanqah Mosque and in the Queen of Abyssinia Street.[39] The land where the church itself was built was donated by Mousa Tannous,[40] also a Protestant, who was interpreter for the British consul in Jerusalem. In 1883 the sect started to think about organizing a national assembly that would supervise religious and social matters in Jerusalem, the rest of Palestine and Transjordan in cooperation with the CMS. At the time of the inauguration of St Paul's Church, the number of Protestants totalled only 136 of whom two were Copts. The rest were previous members of the Orthodox Church and/or the Roman Catholic Church.[41]

The German Missions
The German presence in the Holy Land before the agreement of 6 September 1841 between Frederick, King of Prussia, and the Archbishop of Canterbury was restricted only to sparse visits. In 1853 the Bayt Al-Maqdis (Jerusalem) Society was formed in Jerusalem with branches in several parts of Palestine. This lasted until 1909 when an Arab Lutheran Assembly was formed enabling Arab priests who followed the German Evangelical Union in Jerusalem to hold their own prayers at the Marstan Church in Al-Dabbagha Quarter where the principals of the Syrian Orphanage established for them an elementary school (Schneller School).[42] It is important to mention the Syrian Orphanage here because of the substantial services rendered in Palestine and also in Jordan after 1948. It was established by the priest Johann Ludwig Schneller on 11 November, 1897 and his son subsequently took over the management. It had orphans from both sexes and became famous for teaching crafts that included

carpentry, ironmongery, sewing, printing, pottery, shoemaking and music.[43] It had to stop many of its activities in Palestine after 1948 because of Israeli harassment and moved a great deal of its activities to Amman where it became a multiservice institute in the Marka District north of Amman. It offered all it could to help the residents of Hiteen Refugee Camp who had been forced to move after the 1967 War.

The Germans are credited with establishing the largest hospital in the Old City of Jerusalem, known as the German Hospice, in 1851. Part of its costs was covered by a donation from the Prussian King and the Ministry of Religion in Berlin. They also had the school of Talitha Kumi which was an orphanage for girls that rendered lots of services to the people of Palestine in the same way as other German institutions such as the Augusta Victoria hospital and the hostel known as Almuttala by the Arabs. Building work on the German Hospice started in 1905 using donations collected in Germany following the visit of Kaiser Wilhelm II and his wife Augusta Victoria. On its completion in 1910 it was presented to the Emperor and Empress as a souvenir of their 25th anniversary. The inauguration ceremony was attended by the Kaiser's second son Prince Eitel Friedrich and his wife. This large hospital is still operative today and continues to serve Arab residents. It is run by the Lutheran Union drawing on UN funds via the UNRWA (United Nations Relief and Works Agency for Palestine Refugees in the Near East).

In addition there are churches, monasteries, a hostel and a school for archaeology. There is also Schmidt's College for Girls which was established in 1886 by the German Catholic Society for the Holy Land to educate and train Arab girls up to high-school level. In 1945 the number of girl students was higher than 450, including 70 boarders.[44]

Notes:

(1) Muhamad Farid, *Tarikh Al-Dawla Al-'Aliya Al-'Othmaniya,* Dar Al-Jeel, Beirut 1977, p.278

(2) 'Aref al-'Aref, *Al-Muffassal Fi Tarikh Al-Quds* (Al-Quds – Maktabat Al-Andalus, 1961), p.276 (in Arabic)

(3) Derek Hopwood, *The Russian Presence in Syria and Palestine, 1843-1914: Church and Politics In the Near East* (Oxford, Clarendon Press, 1969), p.48

(4) Ibrahim Qandalaft "Status Quo and Church Institutions in the Holy Land (Syria – March 1969)" pp.18-19 (in Arabic)

(5) Salim al-Sayegh, "Status Quo for Holy Places", (Rome, 1971), *Magazine of the Council of Churches in the Middle East,* (October 1986) p.13

(6) Anton Bertram and Harry Charles Luke, *Report of the Committee appointed by the Government of Palestine to study the situations of the Orthodox Patriarchate in Jerusalem* (Oxford University Press, 1921), p.315

(7) Raphael Hawawini, *A historical glimpse at the Greek Fraternity of the Holy Sepulchre,* (The Committee of Aid and Support for Orthodox within the Jerusalem Patriarchate, 1997) p.132

(8) 'Aref al-'Aref, *Christianity in Jerusalem* (Jerusalem, Roman Orthodox Printing Press, 1951) p.100. And *Al-Muffassal Fi Tarikh Al-Quds,* p.268

(9) Al-'Aref, *Christianity in Jerusalem,* pp.98-110

(10) Ibid, p.118

(11) Al-'Aref, *Al Muffassal fi Tarikh Al Quds* (in Arabic) p.114.

(12) Al-'Aref, *Christianity in Jerusalem,* p.147

(13) Copied from a pamphlet published by the Patriarch and handed to me by Mr George Hazou in Amman

(14) Al-'Aref, *Christianity in Jerusalem,* p.144

(15) Hopwood, *The Russian Presence in Syria and Palestine, 1843-1914: Church and Politics in the Near East,* p.53

(16) Ibid, p.61

(17) Ibid, p.72

(18) Shehadeh and Nichola Khoury, *Summary of the History of the Orthodox Church of Jerusalem* (Jerusalem Printing Press 1925).

(19) Al-'Aref, *Christianity in Jerusalem,* p.48

(20) Ibid, p.48

(21) Al-'Aref, *Christianity in Jerusalem,* p.48

(22) Alessandro Possetto, *Il Patriarcato Latino di Gerusaleme (1848-1938),* (Milano: El Cura di Crociata, 1938), p.30

(23) Al-'Aref, *Christianity in Jerusalem*, p.55

(24) Pierre DeFignoy, *Monsignor Joseph Valerga*

(25) Al-'Aref, *The Detailed History of Jerusalem* (in Arabic) p.531

(26) Ibid, p.530

(27) Pierre Medielle, *The Latin Patriarchate's School of Theology* (Jerusalem, Latin Monastery's Press, 1952) pp.12, 67.

(28) Ibid, pp.531, 532

(29) Al-'Aref, *Christianity in Jerusalem*, p.60

(30) Ibid, p.68

(31) Ibid, p.112

(32) Ibid, p.120

(33) Ibid, p.121

(34) Ibid, pp.148, 150

(35) Rafia Farah, *A History of the Anglican Church in Jerusalem 1841-1991* (Jerusalem, 1995), part 1, p.98

(36) Ibid, p.103

(37) Ibid, p.119

(38) A.L. Tibawi, *British Interest in Palestine, 1800-1901* (Oxford University Press, 1961), p.137

(39) Ibid, p.225

(40) Ibid, pp.115,150

(41) Al-'Aref, *Christianity in Jerusalem*, p.171

(42) Farah, *A History of the Anglican Church in Jerusalem 1841-1991*, p.183

(43) Al-'Aref, *Christianity in Jerusalem*, p.172

(44) Ibid, p.192

CHAPTER V

The Rule of Sultan Abdul Hamid II and the Growing Competition Among the Different Sects

T he rule of Sultan Abdel Aziz, who came to the throne in 1861, ended when he was dethroned on 10 May, 1876 and replaced by Murad V, his epileptic nephew. Murad was, in turn, dethroned and replaced with his youngest brother Abdul Hamid II who was proclaimed Sultan on 31 August, 1876. He started his reign feigning good intentions but in reality he was a cunning person, quite capable of hiding his real intentions[1]. To execute his plans, and influenced by Midhat Pasha, he gave the people a Constitution on 23 December of the same year, "in the same day that representatives of major countries met in Constantinople in a general conference to discuss the conditions of the Sultanate's Christians in an attempt to stop a possible war with Russia which was mobilizing its armies in preparation to fight."[2] With this remarkable trick the new Sultan was able to destroy the opportunities for European countries. He was off to a good start for his reign, raising the level of public affection and trust among his subjects to the extent that the Deputy Armenian Patriarch and the Jewish Rabbi were vehemently opposing the Conference's proposals to protect Christians. They announced that all the followers of both of their sects were willing to defend the honour of the Ottomans. Hungarians, who had been subjects of the Ottoman Empire for many generations, were the most loyal nations to the Ottoman State[3].

The citizens of the Arab countries welcomed the new constitution and the appointment of Midhat Pasha as Prime Minister. They welcomed also the new administrative system for Bilad al-Sham (Greater Syria) through which Jerusalem became a *sanjaq* (administrative region) as a distinct and separate administrative entity. In 1877 Yousef Dhia Pasha al-Kalidi was elected to the Majlis Al-Mabouthan (Parliament) whose mission was to carry out the Sultan's instructions as outlined in the constitution, ensuring that there would be no differentiation between Ottoman subjects regardless of religion and ensuring a wide understanding that all were equal in the eyes of the law. These hopes, however, evaporated when the Sultan, two years later, suspended the constitution and closed down the Majlis Al-Mabouthan. He started to run the Empire according to his own personal whims with complete disregard to the nation. Conditions in Palestine and particularly in Jerusalem worsened in all aspects – agricultural, economic and administrative.[4]

Meanwhile, events were unrolling with important developments for the Orthodox in the Holy City and within the Jerusalem Orthodox Patriarchate in general. Conflicts between Orthodox Arabs and the Patriarchate's Greek priests escalated in 1872 when the Church of Constantinople held a regional Synod which was attended by the four Greek Patriarchs of Constantinople, Alexandria, Antioch and Jerusalem. There they considered the secession of Bulgarians from the Church of Constantinople and confirmed that they saw their independence in running their ecclesiastical affairs as heresy. The Synod declared all Bulgarian bishops excommunicated. However Patriarch Kirellis took a different stand from the other three Patriarchs and expressed his disapproval. When they insisted, he apologized and took his leave saying that he had to follow up on a matter of utmost importance. He confirmed that he had to return to Jerusalem to be there to receive the Russian Tsar Nicholas, who was going to visit the Holy Land, and that he said that he would give the Patriarchs his final decision upon his return. It was said that as he made his excuses in Constantinople, he was threatened by Count Agnativ, the Russian Ambassador who said that unless he followed this course Russia would cut off all revenues from the Jerusalem Patriarchate's endowments in Serbia. [5]

When Patriarch Kirellis arrived in Jerusalem, he found that the Fraternity of the Holy Sepulchre had held a meeting and decided to recognize the legitimacy of the Constantinople Synod and also to dethrone the Patriarch because he refused to comply with the Synod's decisions, and to sever all ecclesiastical and administrative ties with him. The National Orthodox rebelled in support of the Patriarch claiming that the Fraternity was a minority who did not have the jurisdiction to depose him. They proclaimed him the "legitimate Patriarch of the Jerusalemite seat", assisted by the Russian Consul upon the instruction of his country.

The local government intervened, filling monasteries with Muslim soldiers to face those monks who did recognize the Patriarch's right to sit on the Seat as the legal Patriarch, as he was deemed by the government and the people. The Greek monks, in turn, sent a delegation to Constantinople to ask the government to confirm deposing him. Their justification was that he leaned to Russia, enemy of the Ottomans, and was receiving funds from her and that he sought to secure special privileges for her in the Church of the Holy Sepulchre and ultimately sought to provide Russia with a foothold in the Holy Land. Due to the continued animosity and wars with Russia, the Turks were willing to believe such accusations and turned against the Patriarch and approved his deposition. Nazeef Pasha, governor of Jerusalem, was ordered to arrest him and send him to Constantinople, so he left Jaffa on 6 December 1872.

The Fraternity of the Holy Sepulchre then installed Procobius, Bishop of Gaza, as Patriarch, a position he has not well qualified for. He started his tenure by closing the elementary schools and the hospital, something which led the Orthodox to rise up against him. They formed the National Orthodox Society in 1873 which sent a delegation to Constantinople to protest against the closures. Meanwhile, the National Orthodox showed a great sense of unity and courage when they severed all ties with the Greek priests and took control of many monasteries. They also ceased praying in St Jacob's Church in order not to have any contact with the Greek priests within the Church of the Holy Sepulchre. They asked the Russian government to send them part of the revenues from endowments in Serbia to enable them to resist the Greek priests who spent lavishly to confirm and strengthen their position, while they, in contrast, were destitute and could not get back their stolen rights. These attempts, however, did not succeed. The Russian government did no more than allocate ten thousand roubles to be paid annually to the deposed Patriarch Kirellis.

+++

Anyone following these developments will notice that the ongoing struggle between the Tsar's Russia and the Ottoman Empire stoked the fire of conflict between the Orthodox Arabs and the Greek priests of the Fraternity of the Holy Sepulchre. It was the latter who won the round thanks to their cunning and the ample money in their possession. Khalil Ibrahim Qazaqya in his book *History of Jerusalem's Apostolic Church* stated that Greek priests, by dint of their cunning and lavish spending, won over Kamel Pasha, the governor of Jerusalem. Using the same means they were able, in Constantinople, to convince the State to promulgate the law known as Law of the Jerusalem Patriarchate which was ratified during the governorship of Kamel Pasha in Jerusalem in March 1875. However, the Arab Orthodox delegation finally succeeded, to some degree, in conveying the Arab point of view to the Ottoman Empire who, in the same year, deposed Patriarch Procobius, only two years after he had started in post.[6]

It was evident, from the short time it took the State to issue the Patriarchate Law, that the State was wary of continuous Russian interventions in Orthodox matters, especially when Tsarist Russia was forever boasting that it was the protector of the Orthodox within the corners of the Ottoman Empire.

Arab happiness with the new constitution did not last long. Sultan Abdul Hamid, having strengthened his position, deposed Midhat Pasha, the father of the constitution on 5 February, 1877 because he did not want to share power with him. This reluctance was all the stronger since it was Midhat Pasha who had successfully dethroned two Sultans before, and he was, moreover, also publicly and widely acclaimed for his liberal views. The Sultan was only interested in his own safety and was firmly focused on the drive to stay on the throne and to close the doors to the advancing Western liberal tides. The Ottoman State had to confront the war declared by Russia in 1877 – the fourth in the 19th Century – prompted by Russia's desire to seize Constantinople and by her despondence about how successfully the Sultan was likely to carry out political and social reforms peacefully. Sultan Abdul Hamid seized this opportunity to dissolve the Al-Mabouthan Council, giving the green light to oppression and the rule of spies who were to became a major feature of his reign. In short, he turned the lives of people throughout the Empire into misery.

During these decisive events, life in Jerusalem went on otherwise much as usual, with Muslims and Christians enjoying peaceful coexistence in spite of the sizeable number of Jews among them. The Jewish population reached 11,000 in 1870 according to their own estimates – equal to the number of

Muslims (6,500) and Christians (4,500). Meanwhile, Ottoman sources indicated that in 1871 the residents of Jerusalem were as follows: 6,150 Muslims, 4,428 Christians and 3,780 Jews. As the number of Jews increased, they came to have higher demands. They started asking the Ottoman government for more facilities and privileges and resorted to bribery to reach their goals. It was this that made Sultan Abdul Hamid issue an edict in 1882 prohibiting Jewish immigration into the country and banning Jews from buying land there.

When the American consul in Constantinople intervened the Sultan partially retreated on this policy and allowed Jews to visit for religious purposes and to stay in Palestine for a period of three months maximum.[7] They found ways to get around these limitations one way and another, however, and by the end of the century their number increased within the Holy City and they had six synagogues: two for European Jews (Ashkenazi), three for oriental Jews (Sephardim) and one further synagogue.[8]

The local administration within the city started to develop and improve. The municipal council was established in 1863 and all residents participated. In 1875 instructions were issued to organize its affairs and the numbers who voted were 700 Muslims, 300 Christians and 200 Jews. The council included six Muslim members, (one being the mayor), two Christians and two Jews. This political participation in the local government was accompanied by a growth in services activities and strong economic growth generally – evidence of an important development in Jerusalem's life as a mixed community. Even though the available data is not very accurate, yet Warren mentioned in statistics from the late sixties that the number of those working in crafts and industry were 2,132, including 828 Muslims, 801 Christians and 503 Jews.[9]

The Jewish campaign, mentioned earlier, aimed to encourage settling within the Holy Land and to establish a state for Jews in Palestine that, for them, was the Promised Land. Yet this Arab-Jewish struggle was accompanied by another fierce struggle between Russian influences in Bilad al-Sham generally, and in Jerusalem in particular. The Russian Foreign Affairs Ministry had made it clear to the Tsar that the best way to penetrate the Near East was through the Orthodox Church. Once he had been convinced of this point, the Tsar issued a decree approving the formation of The Imperial Palestinian Orthodox Society which in reality became a part of the Russian Foreign Ministry.[10] One of [11] the primary objectives of the

Society was to increase the number of Russian pilgrims to the Holy Land and to encourage educational activities. The number of visiting pilgrims rose sharply from a base of 3,000 in 1900, augmented by repeated visits from the Russian Fleet and from groups of students and monks. This large increase in the number of visitors forced the Society to start a residential project to house the large numbers at a time when accommodation in Jerusalem was in short supply. Managers within the Society noticed the shortage of water within the city, triggered by the fact that its population had tripled since 1851. In 1900 they built twelve reservoirs to collect water, doubling the capacity provided by the municipality for the whole population. To finish this project, the Russian Society also dug a rocky canal 2,000 metres long, supervised by Jerusalem's chief engineer at the time, Engineer George Franjiyyah, of Lebanese origin.

In the field of education, Khetrovo, the first manager of the Russian Society, noticed that the numbers of Orthodox were decreasing substantially. Although they constituted 90 per cent of Christians in the Holy Land in 1840, they became 67 per cent of the total by 1880. While Catholics and Protestants totalled 13,000 with 82 schools, the Orthodox population amounted to 26,000 thousand with only two schools. He also noticed that Catholics were supported by France, Austria, Italy and Spain; Protestants were supported by Germany and Britain while the Orthodox were not supported by anyone aside from Russia. Khetrovo also noticed that Catholics had, in the field of social services, five French Societies and three Italian Societies. At the same time Protestants had eight British Societies and four German Societies. The Orthodox, however, had only the Russian Society. Moreover Greek priests were busy prosecuting Orthodox Arabs and depriving them of their rights, looting the Patriarchate's funds. These bad conditions were, in his opinion, why the Orthodox Arabs were encouraged to petition the Russian Tsar in 1879 asking for his help to prevent the Greeks who came from Constantinople from staying in the Holy Land.[12]

Here we should mention the archaeological excavation that had started in Jerusalem. The objective was to find the correlation between what was mentioned in the Bible and the facts on the ground in the Holy Land. The British were the pioneers in the field and the Palestine Exploration Fund, which was established in London in 1851, began exploration in the area of Biblical Palestine. Excavations were started by Captain Charles Warren in February 1867. He was assisted by Colonel Sir Charles Wilson, historians

Clairmont Jano and Peterwait Derek; Captain Anderson; Captain Stewart; Captain Claude Rene Conder and Dr Chaplin. Their expedition lasted until the end of 1870 and their findings were published by the Fund.[13] Undoubtedly these studies influenced what was called Biblical Studies – a subject which the Zionist Movement used to serve their ambitions and objectives as they started to become more active at the end of the 19th century. We have to mention here that the Ottoman government allowed these expeditions and excavations on the condition that they would not touch the area of Al-Haram al-Sharif or the other Muslim and non-Muslim holy shrines. Agreement with landlords was also a precondition.[14]

These expeditions and excavations led to increased of interest in all things related to Palestine, and to Jerusalem in particular. In April 1882 Prince Albert, the husband of Queen Victoria, accompanied by Crown Prince George, Prince of Wales, had a four-day visit, crossing 585 miles within the Holy Land. In addition to Jerusalem they visited many archaeological sites in Palestine and Jordan. Accompanying them at that stage was a big team headed by Reverend G.F. Dalton and archaeologists Colonel Sir Charles Wilson and Captain Claude Conder.

This educational and archaeological activity was accompanied by activities within the field of health. The Order of St John started, in early 1882, to rehabilitate St John's Hospital, a centre noted for its great services in optics and ophthalmology. The hospital is said to have served patients as early as 1332 when Sir John Mandeville visited Jerusalem and described it in detail[15]. In 1880 the French built the French Hospital known also as St Paul's Hospital, funded by the French government[16]. The Germans built the German Hospital in 1894 and Jerusalemites named it the 'Majidi Hospital' since each patient paid one Majidi (an Ottoman coin or riyal) upon admission.[17] The Russians also built a hospital for themselves and their pilgrims in 1859 in Al-Maskobiyya outside the walls of Jerusalem. In 1917 this was used by the British (when their mandate started in Palestine) as a hospital to treat their staff[18]. Undoubtedly the availability of these medical institutions had a positive effect on the quality of health in Jerusalem and its surroundings. Their availability turned Jerusalem into an important medical centre especially as they included other government and private hospitals such as those mentioned by al-'Aref, including the Moravian Hospital which was established in 1867 by the Moravian Society to treat leprosy (inevitably it ultimately came to be known as the 'Leprosy Hospital').[19]

Notes:

(1) George Antonios, *Arab Awakening: History of Arabs' National Movement*, introduction by Nabih Amin Faris, Translated to Arabic by Naser al-Deen al-Assad and Ihsan Abbas (Beirut, 1962) p.278

(2) Muhamad Fard, *History of the Ottoman Empire 1908* (in Arabic), (Al-Jeel Press, Beirut, 1977) p.346

(3) ibid, p.347

(4) 'Aref Al-'Aref, *Al-Musffassel Fi Tarikh Al-Quds*, (in Arabic) (Jerusalem, Al-Andalus Press, 1961), p.297

(5) Shehadeh Khoury and Nicola Khoury, *Summary of the History of the Jerusalem Orthodox Church*, Beit Al-Maqdis Press, 1925, p.206. Khalil Ibrahim Qazaqya, *History of Jerusalem's Apostolic Church*, edited by Naser Issa Al-Rassi (Cairo, Al-Muqtataf Press, 1924) p.176 and Antoine Bertram, *Report of Jerusalem's Orthodox Patriarchate*, translated by Wadi al-Bustani (Jerusalem, 1925) p.73

(6) Bertram, *Report of Jerusalem's Orthodox Patriarchate*, p.73

(7) Hendricus Jacobus Franken and others. *Jerusalem in History* (English version) edited & translated by Kamel Al-Asali (Amman, Jordan University 1992) p.280

(8) 'Aref Al-'Aref, *Al-Muffassal Fi Tarikh Al-Quds* (in Arabic), p.566

(9) Franken and others, *Jerusalem in History*, p.284

(10) Theofanis Stravrou, *Russian Interest in Palestine, 1882-1914: A study of Religious and Educational Enterprise*, Hidryma Melton Cheersonesou Tou Haimou, 68 (Thessalonoki: Institute for Balkan Studies, 1963), p.127

(11) Ibid, p.154

(12) Ibid, p.63

(13) Palestine Exploration Fund, *Our work in Palestine* (Jerusalem: the Committee 1851) and (New York: the Committee, 1873) the introduction, p.335, C.R. Condor, *The Survey of Western Palestine* (London, Committee of the Palestine Exploration Fund, 1881-1885) and *The Survey of Eastern Palestine: Memoirs of the Topography, Orography, Hydrography Archeology*, London 1889.

(14) Jerusalem Centre of Biblical Studies, *Book of Studies* (Lakeland Florida, 1987).

(15) Condor, *The Survey of Western Palestine*, p.256

(16) 'Aref al-'Aref, *Al-Muffassal Fi Tarikh Al-Quds*, p.459

(17) Ibid, p.459

(18) Ibid, p.458

(19) Ibid, p.458

CHAPTER VI

The Educational Revival in Jerusalem and the Struggle Against the Zionist Invasion

I n previous chapters we discussed the educational activities carried out by various societies in Jerusalem from the middle of the 19th century. Going back to the annual report of the Eastern Scientific Institute (1882) published in *Al-Muqtataf* magazine[1] we find that the population of Jerusalem was 20,000 and that the total population of the Region or district of Jerusalem did not exceed 160,000. Jerusalem was enjoying a big educational renaissance due to the spread of boys' and girls' schools and to the existence of a relatively large number of printing presses. The report discussed in detail the names of those schools, the dates they were established, and the numbers of students and teachers in each together with some notes about numbers of alumni and founders of the schools. It is worth mentioning here that the efforts of the Ottoman government in this field were rather limited. It was largely restricted to Al-Rashdiyya Bureau for Boys, established in 1868, which had eighty students and two teachers, plus seven schools (in reality each simply one classroom) for teaching, reading and writing Arabic. They averaged forty students and one teacher per school.

The schools of the various societies were as follows:

Table 6.1
Number of Teachers and Students in the Various Jerusalem Schools

Number	Name of Society	Number of Male Students	Number of Female Students	Number of Teachers
3	Roman Orthodox Schools	194	100	11
11	Latin Schools	255	510	56
1	Roman Schools	-	1	5
5	German Catholic Schools	239	110	30
4	Society for Spreading the Gospel School	51	79	9
3	Protestant Missionary Schools	66	65	9
3	Armenian Schools	70	40	12
	Jewish Schools	1,575	160	87

The report mentioned that the total number of students in these schools exceeded 3,854 (boys and girls). Without doubt the large number of schools, producing hundreds of graduates, had a great influence in raising the level of education in Jerusalem. Moreover, societies did not neglect the importance of printing presses. The Franciscan monks established their printing press in 1847 followed by the Roman Orthodox printing press in 1851, the Armenian Monastery's in 1866, the English Missionaries' Society printing press in 1879 and six printing presses by the Jews between 1830 and 1870.

This renaissance in education is best represented by the Orthodox Khalil al-Sakakini. He was born in Jerusalem in 1878 and obtained his high school certificate in 1893 from the English College (Bishop Gobath's School). He worked as a teacher all his life in addition to his other activities in Jerusalem and also worked in a great many societies such as the Zahrat Al-Adaab Society, the Al-Ittihad Wa al-Taraqqi Society (Political) and the the Orthodox Fraternal Society. He was also very active in resisting the Greek Clerics of the Orthodox Patriarchate whom he accused of denying Orthodox Arabs their rights. This was ultimately to lead to his excommunication by Patriarch Damianos, the Greek Patriarch of Jerusalem. To express the nationalist sentiment that was to stay with him throughout his life, al-Sakakini established the Dustouriyya (Constitutional) School in Jerusalem in 1909. He was helped by Ali Jadallah, Jamil al-Khalidi and Eftim Moshabbak, all aiming to develop national awareness among students and to prepare national, qualified teachers for the future.[2]

Al-Sakakini was one of the first to highlight the sweeping feeling of danger that overwhelmed Palestinians after they became aware of the Jewish danger. They started to become aware of the international manoeuvres behind the settlement plans and drive to create suitable conditions for a permanent Zionist presence in Palestine. Educated Arabs in Jerusalem and in other parts of Palestine soon rose against this imminent danger. The slogan of their movement was that Arabs, Muslims and Christians were in the same trench and had to defend their identity and their very existence in the land of their forefathers. A group of youths established the Society of Arab Fraternity in 1899, headed by Dawood al-Sidawi with Issa al-Issa, Faraj Farajallah, Eftim Moshabbak, Shibli al-Jamal, Jamil al-Khalidi, Nakhleh Tarazi and Khalil al-Sakakini.[3]

That feeling of danger was very strong but people during the reign of Sultan Abdul Hamid II, could not voice their opinions freely since he was noted for being merciless with spies throughout the Ottoman Empire. One Catholic priest, however, was among the first who pointed to the Zionist desire in Palestine, something that was followed with deep concern by Catholics. The Jesuit Father Henry Lamance published an article in 1899 in *Al-Mashreq* magazine titled "Jews and their settlements in Palestine" in which he mentioned what was being reported in Constantinople's press about Jewish diffusion in Palestine and how the press urged Ottoman authorities to confront Zionist activities. After the article exposed to Jerusalem's public the history of the development of Jewish settlements and societies together with their activities and status and the capabilities of individuals and organizations that supported them, the author went on to warn about Zionists wanting to have a presence in Transjordan. He heard from the chief of Um Qays village (in Jordan) that Baron Rothschild had agents canvassing the area trying to purchase lands and letting Jews farm them.[4]

The conviction these Christian thinkers in Jerusalem believed in, along with their brothers, the Muslim thinkers who specialized in education, was, apparently, that correcting the conditions of education would lead to a comprehensive revival that would repel this enormous threat. While simplifying matters in these terms did not yield the anticipated results, the efforts of Khalil al-Sakakini, and the teacher Khalil Baydas before him, led to the development of a national system of education that introduced change to the Palestine schools' curricula by ridding them of old, traditional methods in transferring knowledge to students.[5] It would be beneficial to provide a list containing names and some data about a number of those pioneers in the education field to give the reader an idea about the services rendered to Jerusalem by them in that era.[6] All of them were born in the 19th century.

- Teacher Wahbatallah Sarrouf (b.1839): manager of the Holy Tomb Press owned by the Orthodox Patriarchate in Jerusalem. He translated Orthodox religious books from Greek into Arabic. Taught Arabic at the Orthodox Musallaba School.
- Teacher Nakhlah Zuraiq (b.1861). He arrived in Jerusalem in 1889 to work with the English Mission. Moved to the management of Boys' Preparatory School where he stayed until his death in 1921. He taught arithmetic, algebra, geometry, logic, sciences and geography, all in Arabic.
- Dr Bandali Saliba al-Jouzy (b.1871). He was noted for being an Arab historian and a linguist. He headed the Arabic Language Chair at Kazan University until the end of World War I. He moved later to Baku University where he taught Arabic until his death in 1942.
- Teacher Khalil Baydas (b.1874): born in Nazareth, moved to Jerusalem in 1908. There he led the first Arab demonstration in 1920 and spoke to the crowds during the Prophet Moses' carnival when he urged them to rebel and abort the Balfour Declaration. The British Mandate sentenced him to death; this was later commuted to fifteen years imprisonment. Upon his release, he refused to work with the British Mandate and taught Arabic at the Bishop Gobath School until his retirement in 1945.
- Mr Khalil al-Sakakini (b.1878): studied at the Zion English School then enrolled at the English College where he was taught by Nakhlah Zuraiq. He later became a teacher and an active member in several societies that aimed to liberate the land from the political influence of the Ottomans and the British and from the religious control of the Greeks. He established a national school that accepted students from all religious factions and paid no attention to matters of religion. Later he participated in establishing Al-Nahdah College in Jerusalem. Throughout his life he was an ardent zealot where the Arabic language was concerned. He died in 1953. We discussed his pioneering role earlier in this chapter.
- Dr Najib Sa'ati (b.1885): Studied at the Orthodox Patriarchate School and later at the Musallaba Institute of Theology where he obtained, in

1906, a degree in Greek literature, philosophy, mathematics and theology. In 1911 he got his doctorate and worked all his life as a professor teaching Greek, Arabic and Latin in Alexandria. He published numerous books, articles and research pieces.

- Mr Iskandar al-Khoury al-Beitjaly (b.1890): born in Beit Jala but lived in Jerusalem after 1908. He taught Arabic and French to boys at St Georges School and Frères College, and to girls at the Russian School. He was famous for the nationalistic poems he wrote.
- Mr. Shukri Harami (b. 1898): He finished his secondary education at the St George's School in Jerusalem and later became a teacher at the Friends (Quaker) School in Ramallah. He left for the USA later where he obtained his BA degree from the University of Indiana. He returned to Jerusalem and worked in the field of education. In 1938 he established Al-Ummah (the Nation) School in Bethlehem; it was widely regarded as a factory producing good men who served society. In 1957 he moved the school to a compound he built in Beit Hanina Village (near Jerusalem).

There were many Christians Jerusalemites who actively participated in the struggle for their freedom against the Zionist invasion, seeking to preserve Arab interests. They were led by Khalil Baydas and Khalil al-Sakakini and included the following:

- Mr George Antonios (b.1892). He was born in Alexandria, Egypt where he had his secondary education. He enrolled at Cambridge University and later returned to Palestine at the end of World War I where he lived as an Arab, very proud of his nation. Although he had worked in the Government of the British Mandate, he testified in 1937 in front of the Royal British Committee. In 1937 he was elected as secretary of the delegation formed by the Arab Higher Committee that represented Palestinian Arabs at the St James Conference, London where he submitted a valued memorandum explaining the Arab point of view. His largest achievement, however, was his book *Arab Awakening* which was published in English in 1939. It was translated into Arabic and published in two parts. He died at the young age of fifty on 21 May, 1942. He was eulogized as a beacon of honesty, integrity and tact, and he would always be included as an important page in the modern history of the Arab nation.

• Dr Azzat Tannous (b.1896): born in Nablus and educated in St George's School in Jerusalem and then at the American University in Beirut where he got his MD in 1918. Back in Jerusalem he opened his private clinic. When the Al-Buraq Revolution erupted in 1929 he closed his clinic and joined the fray. He spent months at the Higher Islamic Council which served as a centre for Palestinian Arab media. He worked diligently to present Arab rights and to fight misleading Zionist propaganda. Dr Tannous continued his struggle for his country and took part in the comprehensive strike of 1936 against Jewish immigration to Palestine. He was invited to join the delegation to London, with Jamal al-Husseini and Shibli al-Jamal, calling upon the British government to put a stop to Jewish immigration. When the Arab Palestinian Bureau was established in London, the Palestine Higher Committee asked him to manage it. He accepted the task and covered most of its expenses personally from his own resources. He continued serving the Palestinian cause from London and Jerusalem until 1964, when the Palestinian Liberation Organization was formed. After organizing its first convention, he was appointed as head of the PLO's office in New York. He spent four years there before returning to Beirut where he retired.

• Mr Antoun Atallah (b.1897): had his elementary and secondary schooling in Jerusalem. He later enrolled at the American University in Beirut until he was called for military service by the Ottomans in 1916. He disappeared after the Arab Revolution, was declared AWOL by the Ottoman authorities, and was not able to return to his land until the British occupied it in 1917. After extensive studies he obtained his Law Diploma from the Palestinian Law Institute in 1924 after which he joined the judiciary where he worked as a judge at the High Court in Jerusalem until his resignation in 1943. A year later he became a noted lawyer defending Arab fighters' rights against the British Mandate Authorities and also became Deputy Mayor of Jerusalem. When Mayor Mustafa al-Khalidi died, the Mandate Authorities appointed a Jew as acting Mayor making Jews an actual majority in the council. Mr Atallah strongly protested and, with other Arab Council members, submitted his resignation forcing the Mandate to appoint a British civil servant as acting Mayor until the British Mandate ended. In 1947 he was invited by the British government to attend the London Conference. He declined due to the difference in opinion among the Arab factions. After the Nakba in 1948 he was successful in preventing the liquidation of the Arab Real Estate Bank and enabled it to open branches in Arab areas to give loans to Arabs to enable them to develop farming and construct buildings. The bank participated in the construction of 70 per cent of all buildings and houses erected with East and West banks in 1957. Mr Atallah was elected to Parliament in 1954, representing Jerusalem. He was appointed to the Jordanian Senate in 1963 and was Jordan's special envoy at the United Nations in New York. He also served as Jordan's Foreign Minister where he actively worked to promote inter-Arab relations and ensured that Pope Paul VI's visit to Jerusalem in January 1964 was a total success. After the 1967 war, when Israel occupied Jerusalem and the West Bank, General Moshe Dayan, Israeli Defence Minister at the time, ordered Atallah's deportation to Jordan due to his intense activities in exposing Israel to the media. After that he devoted his time and efforts to tell the world about the plight of Palestinians who became refugees after the 1967 war.

- Mr. Sami Hadawi (b.1904). He was a self-taught man who joined the Mandate Government of Palestine in 1920. He rose to a position where he managed land assessments. He was deeply affected by the 1948 Nakba. His driving message was: "Most Palestinian refugees are living in unstable conditions. The tragedy of Palestinians lies in the fact that a foreign country gave a homeland to an alien people to create a new state, leaving hundreds of thousands of Arabs homeless." Between 1948 and 1967 he worked in Arab political activities as Land Expert with the International Reconciliation Committee and with the United Nations; between 1955 and 1958 he was the advisor of the Iraqi delegation. He also occupied the position of Public Relations Head at the Arab Information Bureau in New York and established its branch in Dallas, Texas. He headed the Palestine Studies Institute in Beirut (1965-1967), and when the Naksa (the 1967 war defeat) occurred he published his book *The Bitter Harvest* in English in 1967. It was the first book published after that war to discuss the Arab Palestinian cause and its various dimensions. He has 18 books to his credit all dealing with basic sides of the Arab-Israeli conflict.
- Mr Henry Cattan (b.1906): studied at the Frères School in Jerusalem and later at the University of London. He obtained a BA in Law from the University of Paris in 1929 followed by a masters degree in Law from the University of London which enabled him to practise law in the British courts. Returning to Jerusalem in 1932 he was appointed as lecturer at the

Palestinian Law Council between1940 and 1948. He was chosen by the people to defend the Palestinian cause at the United Nations Session of 1947-1948 after which he had to move to Damascus where he continued fighting for the Palestinian cause. He published a valued collection of books in English and French in which he presented the Palestinian cause logically and in depth, urging the world to see the injustices inflicted on the Arabs' main cause and the legal arguments connected to it.

• Mr Emile al-Ghoury (b.1907). He studied at St George's School in Jerusalem and in 1929 enrolled at the University of Cincinnati in the USA where he earned a masters degree in Political Sciences in 1933. Returning home he volunteered to defend the cause and published a weekly paper called *Al-Ittihad Al-Arabi*. It was closed down by the British Mandate Authority nine months later. He partook in political activities and was elected general secretary for the Arab Palestinian Party when it was established in 1935. At the onset of the 1936 Revolution, Mr al-Ghoury was elected to be a member of the delegation that left for London for negotiations. His colleagues were Jamal al-Husseini, Shibli al-Jamal and Azzat Tannous. When the British prevented him from entering Palestine in 1939 after a tour he had conducted in the USA he went to Egypt where he stayed for four years as acting manager of the information office established by the Arab Higher Committee. When he was allowed to go back to Palestine in 1942 he resumed his political activity, restructuring the Arab Palestinian Party that was active until 1946 when the Arab Higher Organization was formed, headed by the Mufti, Hajj Amin al-Husseini, who was detained in Paris at that time. Its members were Jamal al-Husseini, Ahmad Hilmi Abdul Baqi, Dr Hussein Fakhry al-Khalidi and Emile al-Ghoury. In the autumn of 1948 Mr al-Ghoury was elected as general secretary of the National Palestinian Council that met in Gaza and which announced the birth of the All Palestine Government. Mr al-Ghoury worked diligently serving the Palestinian cause, covering the United Nations as head of the Palestinian delegation between1960 and 1968. After a long forced exile he was able to return home where he became an MP representing Jerusalem (uncontested) in 1966. Later he became a minister (twice) in the Jordanian Cabinet. He published a respected collection of books, the last being *Palestine through Sixty Years*, a large opus in three volumes.

The names mentioned in this book are only those who stood out along with their Muslim counterpart leaders in defending the Palestinian cause. Khalil al-Sakakini mentions a meeting he had on Monday 21 September, 1908 with Hussein Affandi Salim al-Husseini and teacher Nakhlah Zuraiq saying: "We mentioned the 'Ulama Society' as Muslims say and we were worried that it aimed to preserve worn out traditions that invoked animosity among people. It dawned upon us that it would be a good idea to create a society of Christians and Muslims to fight the old ghosts and to inoculate people with the constitution and make them taste the new spirit,"[7] the spirit of resurrection and awakening. To confirm this new spirit, researcher Samir Saiqaly writes in an article published in *Religious Studies Institute* magazine in Amman titled "Services of Christians towards the Awakening in Palestine" about the new direction and how to make the message reach people through papers published mainly by Arab Orthodox Christians. Their call was for a new life that would preserve good Arabic traditions while taking on board Western cultural influences that were not in conflict with traditional Arab ethics and values.[8]

Notes:

(1) Report of the works of the Eastern Scientific Institute for 1882-1883 (Al-Muqtataf, year 8) p.533

(2) *The Palestinian Encyclopaedia*, two parts in ten volumes (Damascus, 1984-1990).

(3) Khalil al-Sakakini, *Katha Ana Ya Dunia*, published by Hala al-Sakakini in Arabic (Commercial Press, Jerusalem, 1955) p.48

(4) Ali Mohatheh, "Political currents in Palestine during the awakening Period" in Arabic. A paper submitted to the Second International Conference on the history of Bilad al-Sham p.307

(5) Samir Saiqaly, "Christians' Services towards the Awakening in Palestine before World War I", publication of the Royal Institute for Religious Studies, issue no.1 (2000) p.54

(6) Yacoub al-Awdat (Al-Badawi Al-Mulatham), *Masters of Thought and Literature in Palestine*, in Arabic. (Amman, 1976)

(7) Al-Sakakini, *Katha Ana Ya Duna*, in Arabic, p.38

(8) Samir Saiqaly, "Christians' Services towards Awakening in Palestine before World War I", p.55

CHAPTER VII

Development of Conditions in Jerusalem During the Late 19th and Early 20th Centuries

C onditions in Jerusalem and in the whole of Palestine were getting better for the people due to improvements in the economy and communications and also for the open welcome offered to the increasing numbers of pilgrims visiting Jerusalem. The country by then had a network of roads that facilitated travel by horse-drawn carriages. When the railroad line connecting Jerusalem and Jaffa was inaugurated on 26 September, 1892 it was the start of a new era.

These basic developments were accompanied by a new outlook towards the importance of tourism for the country as a whole. This was evidenced by the many official visits, especially the visit of Kaiser Wilhelm II and his wife Augusta Victoria to Jerusalem in 1898 during the reign of their friend Sultan Abdul Hamid II.

Their visit to the Holy Land started by visiting Haifa, where the royal couple landed, accompanied by an entourage of more than 200. Once they had visited Jaffa the procession moved to Jerusalem via Ramallah, Latroun and the village of Abu Gosh. A whole week was spent in Jerusalem before the royals moved on to visit Bethlehem. The occasion provided the state with the opportunity to extend the appropriate hospitality and cordiality to the distinguished guest and his entourage.

Such visits encouraged pilgrims to come in their droves; their numbers reached 20,000 by the end of the century and increased to 40,000 by 1910.

This led to improvements in the services being offered and to an increase in the incomes of those directly or indirectly involved with tourism activities.[1]

It is important to mention that the population of Jerusalem was still not large; in 1880 it was 31,000 which increased to 42,000 in 1890, 55,000 in 1900, reaching 70,000 by 1910.

The above numbers continuously reminded the Arab residents of Jerusalem of the imminent danger caused by the rise in the numbers of Jews among them as shown in the following chart:[2]

Table 7.1
Residents of Jerusalem in the late 19th century and early 20th century according to their religions

Year	Muslims	Christians	Jews	Total
1880	8,000	6,000	17,000	31,000
1890	9,000	8,000	25,000	42,000
1900	10,000	10,000	35,000	55,000
1910	12,000	13,000	45,000	70,000
1922	13,500	14,700	34,400	62,600

Matters changed after the Ottoman coup d'état that brought the Al-Ittihad Wa al-Taraqqi Society to power in 1908 which had its national Turkish agenda that aimed to "Turkishize" other people within the Empire. That society had among its ranks some *dunmas* who were originally Jews who converted to Islam (in appearance only). The state was affected by the society's bias towards Jews and started to change its policy of banning sale of land. It passed a law that granted societies the right to own land in Palestine. It also enacted another law that allowed the sale of Sultanic land and properties by auction. Through those two laws, Jews were able to buy lands before the start of World War I in 1914.[3]

Despite the increasing Jewish pressure to strengthen settling in Jerusalem, disputes between foreign sects continued within the city: disputes where Arab Christians were only spectators most of the time.

In 1901 a violent controversy occurred between the Roman Orthodox and the Latins that ended with a bloody battle when the Orthodox objected to the Latins' sweeping some of the stairs within the courtyard of the Holy Sepulchre Church. Greek priests suddenly started to throw stones at the

Latin monks who retaliated in the same manner forcing Turkish soldiers to intervene to stop the battle after a great effort. Seventeen French monks were seriously injured while some Roman Orthodox priests met the same fate. What is annoying is that those priests in the midst of that fanatical zeal completely overlooked the nature of Christianity, which calls for tolerance and abhors violence. They allowed themselves to commit those despicable acts within the sanctity of the holiest city in Christendom.

During that period German permeation in Jerusalem depended on the activity of the German consulate in the city and on the strong and developing ties between Istanbul and Berlin. That was especially true after the relations between Istanbul and Moscow were severed after the 1877 war started and after the Russian consul was kicked out of Jerusalem and Russian subjects were urged to leave. All that prompted the Germans to place all Russian subjects and properties under their patronage.

This enthusiasm in purchasing land was accompanied with a similar action by the Kingdom of Unified Italy who tried to imitate major powers at the expense of French influence that diminished after diplomatic relations between France and the Vatican were severed in 1904.[4]

What took Christian disputes in Jerusalem to a new high was the big conflict between the Arab constituents within Jerusalem's Orthodox Patriarchate and the Greek priests who dominated the important positions within the Patriarchate. Added to that was the conflict between the priests themselves who competed for those positions. In 1882 Patriarch Iruthius' horse stumbled near St Stephen's Gate which led to his death. Futhius, who was the head administrator of the Assembly of Jerusalem's Apostolic chair church was elected to succeed him. Ephtimus, the bishop of Bethlehem, due to his hostility with Futhius, objected to his election claiming he was under forty and submitted a formal complaint to his friend Kamel Pasha, the Grand Vizier, in Istanbul and to his brother Sadiq Pasha, governor of Nablus. As a result the government ordered a re-election.[5] An agreement was reached between Orthodox Arab notables and heads of the clergy to appoint Nicodemus, Patriarchal agent in Moscow, as Patriarch of the Jerusalem chair. When he was elected, monks feared him because of his strong personality. True enough he made many reforms within the Patriarchate and started a boom in construction helped by the fact that Russia returned to him four-fifths of the revenues of the Holy Sepulchre's endowments in Serbia and Georgia which amounted to half a million roubles. He also chose the Arab Archmenderit Grasimus Yared as Preacher of Jerusalem's chair which he did perfectly.[6] Intrigues and conspiracies within the Fraternity of the Holy Sepulchre, however, never ceased. In 1890 they accused the Patriarch of siding with the Russians claiming that he wanted to grant them special privileges inside the church of the Holy Sepulchre and threatened to assassinate him. While he was visiting the monastery of John the Baptist in the Jordan valley he was shot and wounded by one of the monks. At that time the Fraternity had closed the Musallaba school of theology claiming shortage of funds (actually to spite the Patriarch) which led to a great resentment among Orthodox Arabs, who due to the government's attitude could not support the Patriarch against the Fraternity of the Holy Sepulchre so he resigned and left for Constantinople. Here we have to mention that despite his integrity, he unfortunately resorted to methods that became customary within Greek Orthodox circles. After his election he visited Damascus where he convinced Orthodox notables there and in Beirut along with local bishops to accept Bishop Grasimus as Patriarch of the Antioch seat. He got his wish after he paid 4,000 Ottoman gold coins (pounds) and Grasimus was elected Patriarch.[7] Orthodox Arabs at the time were moving to bring back the Patriarch's position to the Arab element within the Patriarchate of Antioch and the rest of the East. Nichodemus I, the Greek Patriarch of Jerusalem (1883-1890), Patriarch Joachim IV in Constantinople and the Greek newspapers all considered this election as victory of the Greek element over the Arabic element.

Meanwhile, Patriarch Grasimus was considering himself as if in exile since he coveted the Jerusalem Patriarchate. He often resorted to conspiracies to have Patriarch Nichodemus deposed in order to replace him, with the help of his many supporters within the Fraternity of the Holy Sepulchre.

Upon the resignation of Patriarch Nichodemus I the monks of the Fraternity of the Holy Sepulchre elected Grasimus I (1891-1897) as Patriarch of Jerusalem for which he thanked them profusely. When the bishops of the Antioch Patriarchate turned down his invitation to come and elect his successor, he left for Jerusalem, where he started conspiring again to have another Greek elected as Patriarch of Antioch. He succeeded in installing the Bishop of Al-Tour Spirodon who was of Cypriot origin despite the objection of nationals throughout the empire. He also neglected to answer the demands of nationals within the Patriarchate of Jerusalem. Despite that he failed to satisfy the Fraternity of the Holy Sepulchre, especially the members of the Holy Synod who resented his dependence on Bishop Futhius in all his affairs. When he was afflicted with an incurable disease he went to Paris for treatment and died on his return in 1897.

As customary, fierce competition started for his position. When Bishop Futhius realized that the Fraternity would not elect him he supported the election of Damianos, the Patriarchal Deputy and the Archbishop of Philadelphia who became Patriarch on 15 August, 1897. One of his first decisions was the banishment of Bishop Futhius in order to win the trust of the members of the Holy Synod. He appointed him bishop of Nazareth and continued to back him until he was elected Patriarch of Alexandria at the time he was a member of the Fraternity of the Holy Sepulchre. The reign of Patriarch Damianos I saw the declaration of the Ottoman Constitution of 1908. Article III of the basic law "allowed each sect to establish its own council to oversee the revenues from cash and property endowments and see that they are spent as per the wishes of endowers. Those councils are responsible in front of local government and state councils". Orthodox Arabs formed a sect council (Majlis Milli) that included forty members. They formed a delegation that also had six Arab priests and met with the Patriarch on 15 Septembers, 1908 and announced that the Orthodox sect had formed its own Majlis Milli to execute Article III of the basic law. The Patriarch, however, refused to cooperate which drove the nationals to protest by closing St Jacob's Church.[8] Despite that the monks of the Fraternity were convinced that the Patriarch was not qualified to stand up in the face of the nationalist movement and wanted to depose him. They sent him a warning notice asking him to resign. He refused, so next day they set a trap for him. They reprimanded him very harshly forcing him to exit the session of the Holy Assembly before he formally ended it. They wrote his resignation in the Synod's ledger and followed it with the decision to depose him. They accused him of leaning towards the nationals and meeting with them which incited all Greek churches, without exception, against him. Those developments led to a new complication in the Orthodox case in Jerusalem because of the deep rift between the Fraternity and the Patriarch. The national Orthodox Arabs stood up for the Patriarch when they knew about his deposing. They believed that by acting alone, the Fraternity had encroached upon the rights of the Orthodox. They protested by demonstrating, also sending a large delegation to Istanbul which arrived there in early January 1909.

On 3 January 1909 the Orthodox movement expanded to cover all the country. Nationals occupied monasteries after expelling heads of clergy from them. No doubt the government's indecision and its employees acting in the customary manner made things more complicated, especially with what was known about Patriarch Damianos' love of money and using all means to collect it. In the process part of that overflowed to the pockets of Government employees: those who served his purposes. [9] That man was able to last on the Patriarchate's throne until 1931 bringing deficits and impotence in the capabilities of the Orthodox Patriarchate making it at the bottom of the list when it comes to serving its flock and increasing the prestige of Orthodoxy in the Holy Land. [10]

Economic conditions in the Holy City were adequate. The boom in construction mentioned earlier decreased unemployment significantly. All adjoining towns and villages benefited from that, especially in Bethlehem and Beit Jala which had craftsmen in all branches of construction. The other economic matter which was always on the minds of Jerusalemites, especially the Christians, was religious tourism, where monasteries and convents of various sects competed to build hostels to receive visitors. It is also important to note that a significant part of Jerusalem's residents (Jews) relied for their livelihood (directly or indirectly) on alms and donations collected in Europe.[11] Commerce with its various types was, however, the backbone of economic activity. Goods were imported via the ports of Gaza and Jaffa; they covered all the needs of the population from Europe and Egypt. Meanwhile land roads were the artery that supplied Jerusalem with grain from Jordanian regions. Some families excelled in this business such as: the Batatu, Tleil, Nassar, Abu Suwwan and the Halabi families. They extended their business eastwards and invested in land and property while being very active in the grain business, especially wheat. They also traded in ghee and wool.

We mentioned earlier that Abdul Hamid II's reign was marked with violence and cruelty along with spying on people using 30,000 informers.[12]

Sultan Abdul Hamid's reign lasted from 1876 until 1909 and hence one would not be astonished to see the continued tendency towards nationalist actions among Muslim and Christian Arabs especially since they were alarmed by Jewish settlements and the increasing numbers of Jews arriving from distant countries. They were also dissatisfied with what was going on in Istanbul where Al-Ittihad Wa al-Taraqqi Society reigned supreme and became very powerful within the Ottoman Empire. It asserted its Turkish identity at the time Arabs were complaining about discrimination against them in their areas.

The life of Christians within Jerusalem was directly affected by the European presence there and they sensed the international disputes that could lead, in turn, to disputes among the various sects inside the city, which actually was what caused the Crimean War (1854-1856). The year 1882 could have been a turning point when France and Russia sensed Germany's expansionist intentions when Bismarck, its chancellor, signed a military pact with Austria, with Italy joining in three years later making it a tripartite pact which alarmed the rest of the big powers. Britain, however, refused to join the defensive military alliance signed by France and Russia. This was reversed when Germany started to build a huge fleet, forcing Britain to sign what was called an entente cordiale with France in 1904. It was not an official alliance, yet it undoubtedly founded cooperation between the two countries to rein in German control in Europe. In 1907 Britain also settled its disputes with Russia. Meanwhile the other defensive pact included Germany, Austria and Italy; war was sensed coming anytime.

We have no accurate information about the real feelings of the inhabitants during that period because of their fear of the oppressive government, especially Christian Arabs who were trying to assert their Arab identity at the time Turkish elements were acting in a hostile manner towards all Arabs. Also some Muslim elements stressed the importance of excluding Christians from anything related to the government or the army. Meanwhile, intense conflicts between Orthodox Arabs and the Greek clergy within Jerusalem's Orthodox Patriarchate complicated matters more and more. It seems that Christians at the time were not sure of the Ottoman government's intentions towards them especially when decisions and rulings were bought and sold. They were forced to indulge in these corrupt practices to maintain their livelihood and sources of their income. Al-Sakakini wrote about a meeting he had with a Christian delegation from Jaffa made up of Francis al-Khayyat and Hanna al-Issa. The first was Latin while the latter was Orthodox. They arrived on Saturday 14 March, 1914, months before the start of World War I, to invite Christians to form a political party to preserve the rights of Christians who were a minority in the land. In his journal Al-Sakakini stated the following:

In the evening I was visited by Francis al-Khayyat and Hanna al-Issa. We sat discussing the purpose of their trip from Jaffa. After deliberations I said "If your purpose was political, then I would not go for it because I am, first and last, an Arab. I suggest that we form a national party that contains members from all religions and sects to promote national feelings and to spread a new spirit in all. Then, all those elected to the Mob'outhan Majlis (Parliaments in Istanbul), Muslims and Christians, will all be working in the interest of the country."

Since we never heard about the establishment of a Christian party it is therefore clear that the majority among them did not favour that direction since they were Arabs and did not need such a party. However it is important to mention that Christians in Palestine felt that they were left behind when the Ottoman government failed to appoint any of them for membership of the first Mabouthan Council in 1876 or for the second council.

Representation was restricted to one Muslim delegate, namely Yousef Dhia al-Khalidi while the list of the reappointment in the Mabouthan Council contained – on 24 July, 1908 – the names of five Palestinians:

Rouhi al-Khalidi and Sa'eed al-Husseini from Jerusalem; Hafez al-Sa'eed from Jaffa; Sheikh Ahmad al-Khammash from Nablus and Sheikh As'ad al-Shuqairy from Akko (Acre). Not a single Christian was among them.[13] It was the same in the elections of 1912 when there where five deputies from Palestine, two of them from Jerusalem: Rouhi al-Khalidi and Uthman al-Nashashibi. In the 1914 elections there where six deputies; three from Jerusalem: Ragheb al-Nashashibi, Sa'eed al-Husseini and Faidi al-Alami.

Matters remained the same until 28 June, 1914 when the Austrian Archduke Franz Ferdinand and his wife were assassinated at the hands of Serbian conspirators who resisted the Austrian occupation of Bosnia in 1908. Reacting to that, Austria declared war on Serbia on 28 July, 1914 followed by Germany who declared war on Russia on 1 August, and then against France on 3 August. When German armies entered Belgian soil Britain declared war on Germany on 4 August, 1914 throwing all those countries into the furnace of war. Italy, meanwhile, declared that it would not get involved since the war, for Germany and Austria, was not a defensive one. Later it changed its stance and opted to join the Allies after being Italian territories that were under Austrian rule. As for Turkey, which was looked at by Europeans as a German fiefdom, it signed at the war's onset a secret treaty with Germany and two months later entered the war at the side of Germany. After delay, Greece and Romania sided with the Allies making all European countries involved in the war with the exception of Spain, Holland, the Scandinavian countries and Switzerland. The United States of America stayed out of the war until 6 April, 1917 when President Woodrow Wilson announced, in a special congress session its entering the war "to preserve the principles of peace and justice in the life of the world".

Those successive events turned life in Jerusalem into a harsh one as usual during wars. In Khalil al-Sakakini's journal we see glimpses that changed suddenly in the way that people who saw troops marching to war stood silently, as if strangled, looking solemn and desolate. War taught people thriftiness and even stinginess. A family's daily expenses did not exceed three girsh (piastres), enough for bread, grapes and salad. People became bolder and simpler, as if their nature was changed by hardship.[14] The government, according to Al-Sakakini overburdened people who had to cover the cost of supplies for the military and drove them to protests. When timber was out of stock olive trees were chopped down. The government took over English, French and Russian hospitals; it evicted nuns and monks from convents and monasteries. A curfew was declared from 7 p.m. until morning. Authorities declared the war a holy jihad. On 18 November, 1914 the town crier went out calling people to a public meeting in the courtyard of the Holy Haram to protest against Russia and Britain. The city shut down completely and young Muslims and Christians paraded in the streets carrying banners. They descended on the Haram area, Muslims, Christians and Jews where they listened to a fiery speech delivered by Sheikh Abdul Qader al-Mudhaffar after which they moved to the Russian Embassy where they chanted against the Russian oppressive state and calling for its downfall.

From there they went to the German consulate and were greeted by the consul who delivered a speech in Turkish, thanking the Ottoman nation for its sentiments towards the German nation wishing victory for Germany and Turkey over their enemies.[15]

The war went on with all the misery and shortages it entailed. Visitors (tourists) were few with supplies and staples scarce. Life became difficult and harsh for Jerusalemites regardless of their sects until 9 December, 1917 when the British army entered Jerusalem without any resistance after the surrender of the Turks. The era of fear ended then and a new era of unease and tension started after people heard about the Russians withdrawing from the war in November 1917 and after the Balfour Declaration of 2 November, 1917. Emile al-Ghoury, the Palestinian notable, described matters well when he discussed the social features in Jerusalem towards the end of Ottoman rule. He wrote:

> Consciousness about sectarianism and holding on to local and regional considerations were existing in Palestine. Sectarian division was no barrier in integrating and dealing in all wakes of life. Local considerations destroyed sectarianism. Jerusalem was divided into 'harat' (quarters) that were semi-independent. Muslims and Christians living in the same quarter considered themselves as one group. Jerusalem's Jewish residents had their own quarter and had new areas for themselves outside the city walls. The relations between Muslims and Christians, on one hand, and the Jews were restricted to business and limited personal relations. As a group, however, Jews were never persecuted.[16]

We mention here that al-Ghoury was raised in a non-sectarian environment. He was raised within a house that was saturated with Arab nationalism. An article about him in the *Palestinian Encyclopedia* mentions that this goes back to the Orthodox Movement that started in Jerusalem and then spread throughout Palestine and then to Transjordan. It was an Arab movement par excellence and its realities, motives and developments became a major base that gave birth to the National Movement in Palestine in the 20th century.[17]

The Arabization Movement within the Orthodox Patriarchate in Jerusalem was fully supported by Muslims making Al-Ghoury write "That is the best evidence of the growth of Arab Spirit and Arab feeling in Palestine."

Notes:

(1) Hendricus Jacobus Franken (and others), *Jerusalem in History*, English edition edited and translated by Kamel Jameel Asali (Amman, Jordan University, 1992), p.287

(2) Ibid, p. 279

(3) 'Aref al-'Aref, *Al-Muffassal Fi Tarikh Al-Quds* (Jerusalem, Al-Andalus Bookshop, 1961), p.299

(4) Amin Masoud Abu Bakr, *Ownership of lands within Governorate of Jerusalem (1858-1918)* (Amman: Abdul Hamid Shouman Institute, 1996), p.589

(5) Khalil Ibrahim Qazaqya, *History of Jerusalem's Apostolic Church*, edited by Nasir Issa al-Rassi (Al-Muqtataf Press, Cairo, 1924) p.186

(6) Shehadeh Khoury and Nicola Khoury, *Summary of the History of the Jerusalem Orthodox Church*, Beit Al-Maqdis Press, 1925

(7) Ibid, p.233

(8) Ibid, p.238

(9) Khalil Ibrahim Qazaqya, *History of Jerusalem's Apostolic Church*, (Al-Muqtataf Press, Cairo, 1924) pp.189-190

(10) Antoine Bertram and J. Young, *Committee Report – Jerusalem Orthodox Patriarchate*, translated by Wadi al-Bustani (Jerusalem, 1925), p.47

(11) Franken and others, *Jerusalem in History*, p.284

(12) George Antonios, *Arab Awakening: History of Arab National Movement*, introduction by Nabih Amin Faris, translated by Nasir al-Din al-Asad and Ihsan Abbas (Beirut, 1962) p.175

(13) Khalil al-Sakakini, *Katha Ana Ya Dunia*, prepared for publishing by Hala Al-Sakakini (Commercial Press, Jerusalem, 1955), Robert Devereaux, *The first Ottoman Constitutional Period* (Baltimore, 1963), pp.261, 269 and Hassan Hallq, *The Position of the Ottoman State towards the Zionist Movement, 1897-1909*, (Beirut University Press, 1986), p.300

(14) Ibid, p.71

(15) Ibid, p.83

(16) Emile al-Ghoury, *Palestine Through Sixty Years*, (Dar Alnahar Press, Beirut, 1972) second volume: 1922-1937, p.12

(17) *The Palestinian Encyclopedia* (Damascus, 1984-1990), 10 volumes, Historical Studies, p.795

CHAPTER VIII

The Fall of Jerusalem into the Hands of
the Allies – The Conflict Intensifies

For Jerusalem, World War I ended on 9 December, 1917 when British
troops, led by General Allenby entered the city. Middle and South
Palestine became subjected to direct British military administration until
July 1920. Khalil al-Sakakini sensed the forthcoming resulting developments
and wrote in his memoirs on Saturday, 17 November 1917, a month before
the occupation of Jerusalem:

> Nine days ago the Ottoman Government stated to withdraw
> from Jerusalem since the British army was at its gates. Their
> opinions about the fate of the city or the fate of Palestine.
> Some say it will become English because the English are the
> conquerors and others say it will be attached to Egypt, some
> say it will become free. Some people are sad about that
> Ottoman reign and are fearful for the new one since they are
> familiar with the old. Some traditional Muslims feel sorry
> about the Ottoman state leaving these lands because they
> think this is a blow to Islam and that the British arrival here
> would strengthen Christianity and will promote the
> significance of the cross. There is also a group of misfit
> Christians who await the arrival of the British to strengthen
> Christianity. Regardless of what it is, these days are important

historical days for Palestine, and it waited for generations for such days.[1]

As for Dr Ali al-Mahifidha, he mentioned – after recording al-Sakakini's thoughts – that among those who welcomed the British were those who were influenced by the propaganda by the Great Arab Revolt and referred to the article by Sheikh al-Qalqili, editor in chief of *Al-Kawkab* newspaper and to the poem by Sheikh Ali al-Rimawi in praise of Britain published in the supplement of *Falasteen* commemorating the first year of the occupation of Jerusalem. [2]

The days that followed General Allenby's occupation of Jerusalem brought warnings about the evil brought by Britain's complicity with Zionism and its renouncing promises given by the British government to Arabs headed by the Arab King Hussein Ben Ali when it encouraged them to revolt against Ottoman rule. Arabs in general were shocked when they heard the news published in London's papers on 9 November,1917. Great Britain, through its foreign minister, Lord Arthur Balfour hat sent a letter dated 2 November, 1917 to Lord Rothschild assuring him that "the British Government looks with compassion to the establishment of a Homeland for the Jewish people in Palestine".[3]

Reaction in Palestine to the Balfour Declaration, however, was weak as Dr Ali al-Mahifidha mentions. He cites several reasons, quoting Khalil al-Sakakini; "Arabs were too exhausted and weak preventing them from caring about anything; they assumed that the declaration was issued for military needs warranted by the conditions of World War I."[4] It is fair to mention that Arabs in Palestine, despite harsh conditions and war conditions, did not hesitate to show their opposition to the Balfour Declaration. The Islamic-Christian Society in Jaffa delivered a very strong protest to General Allenby in May 1918 and followed it by a similar memorandum to General Clayton on 2 November 1918.[5]

Palestinian Arabs were eying those developments cautiously after the war ended. Emotionally, they were supporting the Arab government formed by King Faisal I in Damascus. What represented their feelings best was the assembly named The Islamic-Christian Society in Jerusalem. Among its Muslim members were: Aref al-Dajani, Mousa Kazem al-Husseini, Muhammad Yousef al-Alami, Jamal al-Husseini, Sheikh Taher Abu al-Seoud and Joudah al-Nashashibi. Its Christian Orthodox members included: Khalil al-Sakakini, Yacoub Farraj, Elias Mashbak, Antony al-Ghouri and Ibrahim Shammas, and from Christian Latins: Shukri al-Karimi, Butros al-Hallaq and Lutf Abu Suwwan. It also included Shibli al-Jamal, a Protestant. The society's members exceeded forty in number. There were also the the Arabic Club and the Literary Forum who celebrated Arab independence on 9 May 1919 commemorating the Arab Revolt that started on 9 Sha'ban 1334 AH. That was attended by foreign diplomats and British officers. The celebration was ended by singing the anthem which was written by al-Sakakini when he joined the Arab army.[6] The truth is that Palestinians returned and presented a unified, collective view regarding the Declaration when they sent an official delegation to London in 1921 calling for rescinding the Balfour Declaration since it contradicts the covenant of the League of Nations.[7]

Those critical events were going on at the time when the British government was going ahead in carrying out its programme. On 28 December, 1917 – forty days after the British troops entered Jerusalem – General Allenby appointed Sir Ronald Storrs as military governor of Jerusalem.[8] His first task was to ensure necessary staples for the residents of the city who were suffering from hunger. After contacting the general, trucks loaded with flour started arriving from the coast to the city to compensate for the loss of supply from Transjordan which was still in the grasp of the Ottomans. After overcoming this difficulty the new military governor turned his attention to tackling other daily matters. In his memoirs he mentions his visits to all organizations and religious sites including his visit to the complex of the European Jewish Ashkenazim (known in Jerusalem as Siknaj). They only spoke Yiddish (the language spoken by Jews in North Europe); they asked him to supply them with an original copy of the Balfour Declaration. We have to mention that the number of those Siknaj Jews in Jerusalem reached 16,000 while the number of Eastern Jews (Sephardim) totalled 14,000. No one, however, knew the number of the Jews coming from Bukhara who still wore the folkloric clothes they used to wear in their original countries. Numbers of Yemeni Jews were also known. As for the Orthodox Patriarchate, Storrs was received by eight bishops and twelve priests who told him that the Greek Patriarch, Damianos, was previously exiled by the Turks with all other members of the Synod to Damascus. They complained to him about the Turks looting all assets within the Patriarchate and how they could barely save the library, icons and the lanterns. Afterwards he paid a visit to the Holy Haram and sent his greetings to Kamel al-Husseini, who was the Mufti at the time. On the second day Storrs visited the mayor, Hasan al-Husseini who was the Mufti's cousin. There he learnt that Muslims (of the Sunni sect and followers of the Hanafi or Shaf'i subsets) reached about 11,000 in number.

He also visited the two Armenian Patriarchates: the Orthodox and the Catholic. There he discovered that the Armenian Orthodox Monastery (within the Armenian Quarter) complained about the absence of Patriarch Damianos and other members of the Assembly whom the Turks exiled to Damascus.[9] He was also informed that the number of Armenian Orthodox varied between 800 and 1,300. The number of Armenian refugees in Al-Salt (in Transjordan) reached several hundred and they needed food desperately. He heard the same story at the Armenian Catholic Patriarchate where the number of the congregation did not exceed 150 with a small number of refugees while the number of refugees in Al-Salt was 400.

As for the Russians and Germans, they had all left because of the war, leaving the arena wide open for priests and missions that belonged to nationalities of the Allies: Britain, France and Italy. As for the Latins there was Cardinal Camassei, the Patriarch and the monk Ferdinando Diotallevi, the senior clergyman in the Franciscan order. Storrs had to allay their fears by telling both that Protestants were not trying to preach among the refugees by having prayers in English and that they only tried to organize a praying place for them within the monastery provided by the Latin Patriarchate for refugees from Al-Salt where they could pray in their native Arabic.[10]

The military governor of Jerusalem mentions in his memoirs that those who fled the abuse and mistreatment of the Turks followed the British troops who had to feed and house them. Those included 7,000 Armenian, Assyrian, Latin, Orthodox, Protestant and Muslim refugees. [11] The Muslims were at the bottom of the list because of their small numbers. This shows that the Turks were more strict with non- Muslim residents. Generally speaking, residents of the Holy city were not subjected to the suffering experienced by others under Ottoman rule in other areas such as Lebanon.

The occupation of Jerusalem by the British was, undoubtedly, a source of pride for them at a time when the French and Italians felt inferior because they had no part in this great accomplishment. Storrs hinted at the dissatisfaction showed by his colleague in the Anglo-French Mission annexed to the campaign in Palestine. In one of his notices he mentions that Georges

Picot incessantly complained that the French presence was not considered to be on a par with the British presence. He even referred to a letter by Mark Sykes, Picot's colleague of the famous Sykes-Picot Agreement dividing Bilad al-Sham among the Allies, dated 15 December 1917 in which he wrote "I understood from Picot that he was extremely disappointed with his presence and with the general status of the French in Palestine."[12]

When some secular Christians complained about the keys of the Holy Sepulchre being kept in the custody of two Muslim families, namely the Nuseibeh and Joodeh families (a tradition that goes back to 1229 when Sultan Al-Kamel signed a treaty with Emperor Frederick II during the Crusade wars) he told those who complained that he was following the rules of the Status Quo. [13] Here we mention that the tripartite deal offered by the Allies remained valid from the date of the occupation of Jerusalem until the time when the San Remo Conference ended in April 1920. Despite that the triple nationality guards continued at the gate of the Holy Sepulchre (British, French and Italian regiments) until they were withdrawn by common consent in 1922.

There were also other problems between the various sects, and between those sects and the military authorities. Storrs, the military governor tried to dissuade the Franciscan monks from building a church on the ruins of the Justinian church in the Garden of Gethsemane near the Russian Orthodox church since leaving the area empty as it had been for many centuries made people identify better with the life that Christ led in Jerusalem more than nineteen centuries ago. His endeavours were not successful. And the marvellous Gethsemane Church was built in the Garden of Gethsemane. In another instance he succeeded in convincing the sects who shared the shrines, as per the Status Quo, to remove the wall constructed by the Roman Orthodox Patriarch in front of the Iconestas within the Church of Nativity in Bethlehem in the early 19th century using the pretext that it stopped Muslims from desecrating the sanctity of the church. To prevent any of the sects claiming ownership of the place in the future he paid the costs of the wall removal from his own official expenses.

An emergency occurred during an occasion Jerusalemites longed for: Light Saturday and Easter Sunday that followed it. All was prepared and 600 cadres from the army and the police were on guard. One day before Easter Sunday (22 May, 1918) he was surprised by a request coming from the Roman Orthodox asking for the presence of a bishop or an archbishop since the Orthodox Patriarch and other bishops were all in exile in Damascus.

After studying all possibilities it was decided that all celebrations would be presided over by Archbishop Porphyries II, head of St Catherine's Monastery in Sinai. Upon his arrival he was proclaimed Acting Patriarch and managed all the ceremonies. With the military governor, he was able to avoid the problems caused by overcrowdedness, common during such occasions, and the stick blows that fanatic Armenians used to direct at the Master of Ceremonies when all are busy looking at the Holy Light.[14]

While talking about Light Saturday we should mention the old tradition where Orthodox Arabs from the Holy City carry their banners in this day's parades. Al-'Aref mentioned thirteen Arab families whose members had the right to carry their banners, they are:[15]

Suleiman family
Al-Ajrab family
Al-Habash family
Al-Harami Al-Baghl family
Al-Qar'ah family
Kattou'a family
Al-Shamma' family
Katan family
Al-Mahshi family
Abi Zakhariyya/ Shahla family,
Mansour family
Alloushiyyah /Ansara family
Abi Zakhariyya family

The same was mentioned by Yusra Jawhariyyah Urnayta, albeit with simple alteration, in her book *Folkloric Arts in Palestine*. She also mentioned that the Aqrouq family had the right to toll the bells in the Holy Sepulchre Church, while the Patriarch distributes the holy flame, giving one to the sect's priest and another to a member of the 'Slihit' family on behalf of the sect and its Arab members. Another flame is handed to an authorized member from the Armenian sect.

British military rule in Jerusalem was, to a great extent, influenced by the intentions of British politicians, especially Lord Balfour, the foreign minister and author of the famous Declaration and General Allenby, head of the Occupied Enemy Territory Administration (O.E.T.A). Storrs' biography clearly shows the extent of their bias towards Zionism and their blatant violations of the Status Quo rules. As a military government, their basic mission was to administer the territories as in Egypt where English was used as an official language with Arabic translation of all issued laws and instructions dealing with important minorities like Jews, Europeans, Armenians etc. Yet the situation in Palestine, due to British collusion, was different. All orders and instructions were issued in Hebrew as well as in English and Arabic.

Trying to justify this violation of military traditions, Storrs confirms that the Balfour Declaration, which was issued on 2 November, 1917 and which was unanimously accepted by the world before the birth of the League of Nations and the issuance of the Mandate document, gave the government the right to deal with Zionism on this realistic ground.[16] No doubt this peculiar situation was noted by Arab leaders, mainly in Jerusalem. Towards the end of 1918 they called for an Arab convention to be held in Jerusalem. Delegations arrived on 25 January, 1919 aiming to discuss the fate and affairs of Palestine. Authorities, however, were able to create many obstacles to prevent the convention, stopping the formation of a public opinion in Palestine and stopping Palestinians from having selected people to represent them. Hence Arab attention turned towards the activities of the Islamic-Christian Society in Jerusalem which had forty Muslim and Christian members and which called for the formation of the Arab League with Palestine as a member. It also called to accredit Prince Faisal Ibn al-Hussein as the representative of the Arab League in the Peace Conference.[17]

In the face of these lame positions from the Arab side, there was feverish activity on the Zionist side resulting in the appointment of Sir Herbert Samuel as High Commissioner for Palestine on 30 June, 1920.[18] His reign and the reigns of his successors in the British Mandate of Palestine were a continuation of the steps prepared by the British government to implement the Balfour Declaration and turn the country into a national homeland for Jews.

The Christian Arab presence in Jerusalem during those vital events was suffering from a clear absence from the stage of events. The military government's main interests were the Jews, followed by maintaining good relations with the French and Italian presence in the Holy Land via the

Vatican in Rome and the Patriarchates and monasteries in Jerusalem. As for Eastern Churches, they were suffering from great difficulties including the large numbers of Christian refugees and the absence of the leadership of the Greek Orthodox Church and the Armenian Orthodox Church, who were in exile in Damascus. They also lacked any organization for the national Orthodox, who constituted the majority of the Christians, to unite them and provide them with leadership that could channel their efforts to get back their rights which were stolen by Greek priests, and to support the national struggle against the conspiracy of turning Palestine into a Jewish homeland.

National feeling, however, found an outlet within the ranks of Palestinian immigrants in America. In a book published in 1919 by the Palestinian Society Against Zionism in New York, managed by Hanna Salah, from Ramallah, and a graduate of the American University in Beirut and Harvard University, we find a series of articles written about Palestine and its cause by a group of young Palestinian immigrants mostly from Jerusalem, Ramallah and Bethlehem.

The book's introduction gave a historical glimpse about "Palestine: its populace and who they are" by Dr Philip Hitti, professor of Oriental History at Columbia University, New York. He pointed to the multi origins and races caused by waves of increase in population. He confirmed that no other spot in the world gave what Palestine contributed to religion and civilization given its size and small population. He presented research about its geography, agriculture, commerce and industry and touched on the subject of Jewish immigration to Palestine which strengthened the Jewish foothold in Palestine.

There was an article by Yacoub Handal about the mother of pearl industry in the Holy Land, followed by an article about manners by Khalil Tawtah. Victoria Tannous wrote about the social position of women, while Dr Fouad Shatarah wrote about health reform. On politics the book had five chapters with the following titles: "We and the Zionists" by Dr Najib Katbeh; "The Zionist Movement: Pros and Cons" by Habib Katbeh; "The Best Means to Resist Zionists" by Mughannam Mughannam; "Between Syria and Palestine" by Dr Rasheed Taqi-Addin; and "The Big Question: Are we a Nation?" by Dr Philip Hitti. It is worth mentioning that Mughannam appealed to Palestinians to get ahead of Zionists in all spheres of work. He listed ten fields of work and ended by calling for a new law to curtail immigration. As for Hitti's article, it revolved around Syria "which does not have a national or a religious unity. The language unity, which is more important, is there. Hence, we are not a nation but the material needed to turn us into one is ready and available, we only lack the will." The book was concluded with an article by Dr Saleem Shihaddah George, the former editor of the *Arab Gazette*, titled "A view towards the future of Palestine" in which he discussed the dimensions of the underlying danger confirming that "we must not forget that Palestine's future depends on its people and now they care about it. It depends on their looking forward and using the principles of correct science."[19]

We mentioned earlier the difficulties that faced the Orthodox Patriarchate in Jerusalem, headed by Patriarch Damianos who had returned from his exile in Damascus in 1919 after the war ended. His policies of squandering money led to overburdening the Patriarchate with massive loans totalling 556,000 pounds sterling even after selling many of the Patriarchate properties in Central Europe,[20] which made Orthodox Arabs and the Greek priests rise in protest. However, the Greek priests' attempt to depose the Patriarch due to conflicts they had with him, was met with total refusal by the Orthodox Arabs who resisted the Greeks attempts to dominate the affairs of the Patriarchate and after much skirmishing the deposing was thwarted. On 27 of August, 1919 the representative of the Greek Bank arrived to negotiate with the Patriarchate the loan it requested to repay its massive debt, at 3 per cent annual interest. As a collateral, the Patriarchate had to mortgage its properties in Palestine (excluding the holy shrines) until the loan was fully repaid with interest in installments for many years.[21] With this the Greek government became directly involved in the Orthodox dispute in the Holy Land after years of working behind the scenes. Despite the fact that Orthodox Christianity in the Holy Land is in reality a national Christianity in Palestine, being an Eastern church in an eastern country. [22] Yet the Greek element – public and official – did not change its stance despite Arabs being the majority. To confirm this we can go back to the population figures as per the 1922 census in Jerusalem showing:

Muslims	13,413
Christians	14,699
Jews	33,971

Later numbers increased and on 1 April 1945 became:

Muslims	30,630
Christians	29,350
Jews	97,000

Distribution per area: 33,600 of Arabs within the old city and 31,500 in the new area outside the walls. The Jews had 2,400 within the old city and 97,000 in the new city. [23] It is clear that the majority of Christian residents were Orthodox Arabs.

Matters between Arab nationals within the Orthodox Patriarchate, and the Greek priests were never calm. Complaints never ceased which prompted the British High commissioner, Sir Herbert Samuel, to form a higher committee on 17 January, 1921 composed of Sir Anton Bertram, senior Judge of Ceylon, and Mr Harry Charles Luke, the deputy of Jerusalem's military governor, to search for the existence of an authority per Orthodox church Law that can issue judgements/rulings for those disputes and what are the procedures needed to set things straight. Another objective of the committee was to determine the best methods to repay the Patriarchate's loan. Archmenderit Timotheos Themeles (who later become Patriarch of Jerusalem), Yacoub Farraj and George Skiksek were appointed as committee secretaries.

It is ironic that this high commissioner who was noted for his complete bias towards Britain and the Jews and who took many decisions that paved the way to establishing the Jewish homeland, as per the Balfour Declaration, and to establishing the Jewish State[24] was the same who formed a second higher committee on 27 February 1925 composed of Sir Anton Bertram and Mr J.W.A Young to study the necessity of revising the Sultan's decrees of 1875 and to check the guarantee of the rights of Orthodox Arabs to be members of the Fraternity of the Holy Sepulchre. This committee was also to look into establishing mixed councils within the Jerusalem Patriarchate that included clerical and secular members and their jurisdiction. The committee also was supposed to study any disputes between Orthodox Arabs and the Orthodox Patriarchate in Jerusalem.[25]

All this made the clear Arab Orthodox case enter into futile arguments but one that kept public opinion in Jerusalem and in Palestine busy for many years.

Chapter VIII

Notes:

(1) Khalil al-Sakakini, *Katha Ana Ya Dunia*, prepared for publishing by Hala al-Sakakini (The Commercial Press, Jerusalem, 1955) p.90

(2) Ali Mahafidha, "Political trends in Palestine during the era of awakening", a paper submitted to the second international conference of the History of Bilad al-Sham, pp.310-311

(3) *The Palestinian Encyclopadia*, 2 parts in 10 volumes (Organization of the Palestinian Encyclopaedia, Damasucs, 1984-1990), volume 1, p.416

(4) Ali Mahafidha, "Political trends in Palestine during the era of awakening", p.310

(5) Al-Sakakini, *Katha Ana Ya Dunya*, p.138

(6) Ibid, p.182, and *The Palestinian Encyclopaedia*, p.65

(7) *The Palestinian Encyclopaedia*, p. 417

(8) Ronald Storrs, *Orientations* (Nicholson and Wilson, London, 1943), p.285

(9) Ibid, p.280

(10) Ibid, p.295

(11) Ibid, p.295

(12) Ibid, p.277

(13) Ibid, p.297

(14) Ibid, pp.306-307

(15) 'Aref al-'Aref, *Al-Muffassal Fi Tarikh Al-Quds*, (Al-Andalus Bookshop, Jerusalem, 1961), p.521

(16) Storrs, *Orientations*, p.301

(17) Al-Sakakini, *Katha Ana Ya Dunya*, p.165

(18) Storrs, *Orientations*, p. 337

(19) Hanna Salah, Palestine and renewing its life, (The Palestinian Society against Zionism, New York, 1919) pp.161, 199

(20) Shehadah and Nichola Khoury, *Summary of the History of the Jerusalem Orthodox Church*, (Beit Al-Maqdis Press, 1925) p.296

(21) Anton Bertram and Harry Charles Luke, *Report of the Committee appointed by the Government of Palestine to study the affairs of the Orthodox Patriarchate in Jerusalem* (Oxford University Press, 1921), p.191

(22) Storrs, *Orientations*, p.407

(23) Al-'Aref, *Al-Muffassal Fi Tarikh Al-Quds*, p.430

(24) Sahar al-Hinaidi, *The Lost Trust, Sir Herbert Samuel, Zionism and Palestinians* (London, 2000)

(25) Anton Bertram and J.W.A Young, *Committee Report, Jerusalem Orthodox Patriarchate*, translated by Wadi al-Bustani (Jerusalem, 1925) p.1

CHAPTER IX

Development of Society in Jerusalem Between 1917 and 1967

T he British Mandate over Palestine was the start of a disaster that befell Arab rights and Arab existence (Muslim and Christian) in the Holy Land. All participated in trying to prevent forthcoming dangers in a way that gave Muslim-Christian fraternity a special quality as a distinctive mark in human history during the 20th century. The Arab-Palestinian Conference which convened seven times between 1919 and 1928 is considered as a national institution similar to parliaments in a country where its Arab sons were deprived from choosing their delegates because of British dominance as per the Mandate document. We note here that electing delegates to this conference was not done according to specific standards but through Islamic and Christian societies and other popular organizations in Palestine. Delegates' numbers to the sessions of the conference varied between 27 and 227 delegates from Jerusalem and other Palestinian cities and regions, and included a number of politicians who had high ranking positions during Ottoman Rule, and members of political societies who later became members in national Palestinian societies.[1]

They also included a number of Christians who actively participated in the agenda of this conference and other conferences as well as in all other national activities. The executive committee, headed by Mousa Kazem al-Husseini remained until 1934 when it dissolved itself after which the Mufti, Hajj Mohammad Amin al-Husseini became the leader of the Palestinian National Movement. We have in the articles and books of Emile al-Ghoury, who became a pillar of that movement, a comprehensive record about that period and about Arab resistance to British bias and Jewish settlers.[2]

The previous chapters saw many mentions about the Zionist invasion of Palestine during the Ottoman Rule and the aid it started getting after the country was occupied by Britain, the issuer of the Balfour Declaration. Those political situations had a great impact on the march of the church which had special ties with Britain, the Protestant church in the Holy Land. "While Bishop Blyth was working within a Turkish Empire that did not sympathize with his work Bishop Maciness (bishop of Jerusalem 1918-1931) found himself under the authority of a very sympathetic British government. Still he faced continuous problems and difficulties as a result of the British Mandate policy in Palestine which aimed at establishing a Jewish homeland in Palestine based on the Balfour Declaration".[3] The relationship between the Anglican Church in Britain and the Protestant Church in Jerusalem led to a strong reaction among Arab Protestants who felt betrayed by the implementation of the unfair British policy that supported the Jews without limits. That is why we see Protestant Palestinians as extremely enthusiastic supporters of the National cause and as leading activists in political, social and economic fields. Among their pioneers were Shibli al-Jamal, Dr Azzat Tannous, Fouad Saba, Bishop Elia Khoury and Bishop Sameer Qafiti.

As for other Christian sects in Jerusalem, the Orthodox were busy with their internal conflicts between the Greek priests and Patriarch Damianos on one hand, and between the Greek element and the Orthodox Arabs on the other. All this led to the formation of a strong tie between the Orthodox Arab revival and the Arab National revival, on the basis that both were liberation movements, the first against Greek control and the second against British occupation. In previous chapters we discussed at length the Orthodox figures who reinforced Muslim-Christian national solidarity in all aspects. Regrettably the political and military situations during the Ottoman era, the British Mandate, the union with Jordan and under Israeli occupation were all against liberating Orthodox Arabs within their Patriarchate in Jerusalem for reasons and factors we cannot discuss in this research. This national issue that has occupied public opinion in Jordan and Palestine since 1872 is still a cause for crucial conflict since it deals with human and religious rights in modern times and, due to the significance of lands and properties the

Patriarchate owns in Palestine, especially in Jerusalem, Israeli expansionist and settlements programmes.

Israel has succeeded in gaining control over a great portion of those properties and is still trying to own whatever remains in the grasp of the defenceless Jerusalem Orthodox Patriarchate.

We move on to discuss the Catholic sects led by the Latin denomination. Their religious affairs were controlled by the Latin Patriarchate in Jerusalem which was headed by Latin Patriarchs coming from Rome who, because of their nationality and loyalties, were driven by the Vatican's policies that were concerned with guarantees to the freedom of worship, pilgrimage to the holy shrines and the preservation of Catholic endowments run by monasteries under supervision. It is evident that the main concern of local Catholic churches at the time concentrated on increasing the numbers of the Catholic congregations. That was successful due to the great efforts to convert Orthodox Arabs to various Catholic denominations by admitting their children to Catholic schools and by showing leniency and compromise in certain social matters such as marriage between cousins which was not allowed within Orthodox Churches. Some detailed statistics published in a book by the Latin Patriarchate about its history between 1848 and 1938 showed the numbers of Christians in Jerusalem in the early thirties of the 20th century. We will show these underneath due to the importance of their details while noting that all Eastern Churches were described as Dissident while all Protestant Churches were dubbed Protestant. All these were combined in one list while Catholics were in a separate list. Christians amounted to 25,000 persons, Muslims 30,000 while Jews totalled 80,000 in number. [4]

Table 9.1
Numbers of Christians in Jerusalem according to their sects

EASTERN SECTS

Sect	Number
Roman Orthodox (Greci Dissenti Ortodossi)	8,000
Jacobite Assyrians (Siriani Dissenti Giacobiti)	700
Gregorian Armenians (Armeni Dissenti Gregoriani)	3,000
Copts (Copti Dissenti)	100
Abyssinians (Abissini Dissenti)	100
Anglicans (Anglicani Protestanti)	3,000

110

Presbyterians (Presbeteriani Protestanti)	100
Lutherans (Luterani Protestanti)	200
Templars (Templari Protestanti)	2,000
Adventists (Avventisti Americani Protestanti)	500
Quakers (Quakeri Americani Protestanti)	500
Total	18,200

WESTERN SECTS

Latins (Cattolici Latini Romani)	5,985
Roman Catholics (Melchiti Greci Cattolici)	272
Armenian Catholics (Armeni Cattolici)	300
Assyrian Catholics (Siriani Cattolici)	120
Chaldeans (Caldei Cattolici)	50
Total	6,727

It is important to note, when studying this table, that the numbers of the Roman Orthodox have decreased during the 19th century because of preaching by missionaries when a sizeable number of Orthodox Arabs converted to other churches because of the conflicts between Arabs and Greeks and also because of the corruption that reigned supreme within the Roman Orthodox Patriarchate.

The following facts throw light on the true picture of the conditions of Christian sects during the period that followed the end of the British Mandate over Palestine:

- The Roman Orthodox are Arabs in majority with about five per cent Greeks – including those who were born in Palestine and those who arrived to stay, especially priest members of the Fraternity of the Holy Sepulchre or their students.
- The Armenians, Copts and Abyssinians were the descendants of families that resided in Jerusalem from different times. Most arrived for pilgrimage but stayed and became Jerusalemites.
- All other Protestant Churches, i.e. Anglicans, Presbyterians, Templars Adventists and Quakers, are new sects that grew due to missionary efforts starting in the mid 19th century. Although they included a number of non-Arabs most of the followers of those churches were Orthodox Arabs

111

who converted because of their dissatisfaction with the Greek spiritual hierarchy. Providing education for their children was a big factor in convincing them to convert. The Quakers' success in Ramallah (where they have an excellent school) could have been the primary factor in the increase in the number of immigrants to that area from the US.

- As for Latins, most of them were originally Orthodox Arabs who converted because of missionary preaching and because of educational and schooling opportunities offered to their children to study in schools opened by Latins throughout the country. We have to mention that the percentage of foreigners among Latins was rather high; it could have reached 20 per cent due to the large numbers arriving from Latin countries such as Italy, France and Spain for religious reasons. It is important to note that Latin influence in the areas of Jerusalem, Bethlehem and Beit Jala led to a rise in the immigration from South American countries.

- It is astonishing that missionary campaigns continued preaching among the Orthodox Arabs for long periods and were not met by any noticeable resistance from the Greek monks who controlled the Orthodox Patriarchate and who were busy with their own disputes and trading corruption charges among themselves. It is accurate to say that the numbers of the flock of the Patriarchate of Jerusalem would have been fewer were it not for Russian efforts that prevented a larger number of Orthodox Arabs from converting to the Protestant and Latin faiths during the 1880s. That was when the Russian Society worked diligently to establish schools and organizations, not only in Jerusalem but throughout Bilad al-Sham (Syria, Transjordan and Palestine).

The nature of the conflict between Arabs and Jews and their British allies made it clear that it was a crucial one. This made Palestinians rally all their forces. They expressed their protests and dissatisfaction through meetings, demonstrations, sending delegations and holding conferences. Religious figures did not hesitate to participate in all those activities especially after Hajj Mohammad Amin al-Husseini, the Mufti of Palestine and chairman of the Arab Higher Committee, assumed leadership. He was elected as Mufti of Palestine in 1921, and as head of the Higher Islamic Council in 1922 for many years until he died in 1974. During that period many figures came into the limelight. One of them was Gregorios Hajjar, the Roman Catholic bishop who was noted for his eloquence and for being one of the best orators of the time. Palestians nicknamed him " the Bishop of Arabs" in 1924 when he delivered a speech in front of Sharif Hussein bin Ali, king of Hijaz, congratulating him for the fatwa issued by Hajj Amin al-Husseini naming him Caliph of all Muslims. Bishop Hajjar said:

> In my name, and on behalf of Palestinian Christians who I have the honour to represent, I stand in front of you to declare that we, the Christians of Palestine will stick to our land and will defend it. We are the original owners of this land and have lived with our Muslim Bretheren in peace and love for many centuries. We want to continue doing so to confront and defeat the conspiracies against our country. Since the days of Caliph Omar Bin Al-Khattab Muslims have been treating us like brothers and we don't want anything to change that.[5]

When the Resistance Movement increased its fights against the leakage of lands to Zionist hands, a conference was held in Jerusalem on 7 August, 1934 for Muslim sheikhs where a fatwa was issued denouncing any Arab selling any land to Zionists and declaring him as a renegade against Islam. On 29 August, 1934 a similar conference was organized by Christian Orthodox Arab clergymen in Jerusalem which was attended by 73 Orthodox clerics. It lasted for three days at the end of which they declared that they stick with the Palestinian National Covenant of 1922. They also declared their refusal to submit to the laws and regulations issued to weaken Arabs and force them to sell their lands. Resistance was declared as a duty and an obligation for all Arabs. The conference also decided that "any Christian selling land to Zionists or acting as an agent in the sale will be considered as a traitor to his religion and country and would not be buried in Christian cemeteries".[6] All those movements accompanied the popular uprisings that started in 1920, followed by the 1929 revolt then by the 1936 revolution that lasted until 1939, stopping only because of the outbreak of World War II.

It is only natural that Palestinians sensed the importance of the economic side when their lands were targeted, threatening to uproot them from their towns and villages. Trying to defeat that plan they tried to activate their meagre and limited resources at a time when the Zionist Movement enjoyed unlimited support from world Jewry. Jerusalemites were primarily concerned to promote tourism which had been a good source of income for them for the last two centuries with all that was attached to it: hotels; arts and crafts trade; travel and transport; and exchange of various goods in demand by pilgrims and visitors.

Here, it is important to mention the names of the Christian families who were involved in various activities during the thirties and forties of the 20th century: [7]

• **Hotels and hostels:**
Lorenzo, Murqus, Mansour, Karahshedh, Sawalha, Salah, Almaza, Hadad, Naser, Rafidi and the Vesters (owners of the American Colony Hotel).

• **Pharmaceuticals:**
Halabi, Atallah, Said, Murqus and Mavromichaelis

• **Auto trade and spare parts:**
Homsi, Mansour, Marto and Noman

• **Food and staples:**
Zafriades, Ishtaklef, Stragalis and Khamis

• **Auditing and accounting:**
Fouad Saleh Saba, George Khader and Hanna Bawwab

• **Travel and Transport:**
Zananiri, Sahhar and Sinunu

• **Souvenirs, arts and crafts:**
Mio, Dhabour and Shagouriyyah

• **Building materials:**
Qattan, Mahshi, Marroom and Minneh

• **Printing presses and book distribution:**
Halabi, Dardarian, Lawrence (Lorenzo) and printing presses within monasteries

• **General trade:**
Albina, Freij, Qalbian, Qattan, Kittaneh, Minneh, Yaghnam, Hamarneh, Tleel and Deeb

• **Insurance:**
Arabia Insurance company, founded by Basem Amin Fares, plus agents for various British and Canadian Insurance companies

• **Ice making and carbonated soft drinks:**
Mumtaz, Khamis and Shater

• **Grain milling:**
Kalayjian

• **Mechanical Works:**
Nassar

We note there was no important or heavy industry in Jerusalem. This is due to the nature of the Holy City and to the non-availability of agricultural land and natural resources around it making its residents direct their attention to promoting tourism and pilgrims' visits.

That economic activity was, however, accompanied by cultural activity despite the huge difficulties imposed by the Mandate on Arab citizens coupled with the harsh conditions imposed by the war which had lasted for four exhausting years. There is no doubt that different churches and monasteries with all their social, cultural and benevolent activities played a great role in this field. The Orthodox Arab Revival, which resisted trying to regain the Arab rights previously usurped by Greek monks, stood tall by establishing the United Orthodox Club which played a significant role in Jerusalem's national and social life in the 1940s. The Palestinian Orthodox Society was also established and had branches in various Palestinian cities and towns. At that time the Palestinian press started publishing numerous articles that helped ignite the spirit of nationalism among Arabs alerting them to the colonial attack that presented a real danger to all without exception. Meanwhile the revolt was growing day by day. When Andrews, governor of Galilee, was assassinated in October 1937, the British authorities hunted down the members of the Arab Higher Committee and sent a

115

number of them to exile in the Seychelles. They included Fouad Saba who only returned, with his compatriots, on mid January 1939. Other members sought refuge in Lebanon and Egypt. Emile al-Ghoury had to escape to Beirut with many other nationalists.[8]

On 7 February 1939 the Round Table conference was held in London (Britain invited Palestinians and Arab countries to attend). It was opened by Prime Minister Neville Chamberlain. Among the participants were: Malcolm McDonald, the British Minister of Colonies; Prince Mohammad Abd al-Munim crown prince and head of the delegation of Egypt; Prince Faisal bin Abd al-Aziz as head of the Saudi delegation; Prince Saif al-Islam Abdallah head of the Yemeni delegation; the prime minister of Transjordan and the Iraqi prime minister. The Palestinian delegation was headed by Jamal al-Husseini with the following as members: Amin Abdul Hadi, Ragheb al-Nashashibi, Amin al-Tamimi, George Antonios, Hussein al-Khalidi, Yacoub Farraj, Abdul Latif Salah, Alfred Rock, Yacoub al-Ghusain, Fouad Saba and Mousa al-Alami.[9] We note here the large number designated for Jerusalemites. They were represented from the Muslim side by Jamal al-Husseini, Ragheb al-Nashashibi, Hussein al-Khalidi and Mousa al-Alami. From the Christian side they were represented by George Antonios, Yacoub Farraj and Fouad Saba.

Unfortunately the conference's sessions were ended prematurely by the British government to enable it to act individually by declaring the results and publicizing its new policy contained in the White Paper of 17 May 1939 which was met with refusal by Arabs and Jews alike.[10]

When we ask about the conditions of coexistence between Muslims and Christians under such circumstances, we conclude that someone like Emile al-Ghoury, Orthodox Jerusalemite, and his compatriots such as Khalil al-Sakakini and George Antonios would be the best to describe the prevailing conditions among Palestinians at the time of the British Mandate. In an essay titled "The Policy of divide and rule" al-Ghoury describes in detail the British conspiracies to shatter Muslim-Christian unity by promoting and strengthening the ugly sectarianism: "they thought that Christian Palestinians would support the British Mandate and its policy since Britain is a Christian state with its king as protector of the Faith". Therefore, the British thought that it was impossible to have Christians defying the policy of a Christian state. Among the factors that made the British believe this was its assumption that Christians and Muslims in Palestine clashed with each other and hated each other due to religious and opinion differences. The British also assumed that the Christians, being a minority, sided with the Jewish minority. In addition to this wrong assumption and to the oversimplification of matters, Britain thought that it had many reliable friends in the region due to the schools and missions it established there before World War I when it started trying to convince Christians that it was a Christian state whose duty was to protect their interests and look after their rights and holy shrines. Britain's efforts in this respect were, however, in vain, and citizens of Palestine retaliated by forming Islamic-Christian societies to stand against British/Jewish policies. The apparently sectarian name was deliberately chosen for the leadership of the national movement to stress the depth and strength of the binding ties between Muslims and Christians.[11]

Al-Goury mentioned several attempts by Britain to instigate sedition all of which were thwarted due to the prevailing national feeling. Thus the unity between Muslims and Christians overcame all attempts and endeavours to break it up.[12]

Here we have to stress the national feeling and activities that Orthodox Arabs aspired to in that period through forming the Orthodox Union Club on 20 December, 1941 to activate their political activities which were resisted by the Occupation Authorities using all possible means.

When they applied to form that club they declared that its objectives were "religious, charitable, social, cultural and athletic; objectives that benefited the Orthodox sect and the Arabs Society". They also declared that the club "will never interfere in political matters", all at the time when the club was playing host to a bevy of leading authors and thinkers from the Arab world who gave lectures on Arab unity and Arab achievements in battle and in the arts and sciences with lectures about Arab civilization in their countries as well as in central Asia and Andalucia. The club secretly opened its doors for non- Orthodox figures to become supporting members: "the administration has the right to elect any individual, who performed useful services to the Arab Society, to be an honorary member, placing no limits on the number of such members". Many Muslims became members as a result. [13]

Notes:

(1) *The Palestinian Encyclopedia*, volume 2 (Damascus, 1984-1990), pp.368-375

(2) Emile al-Ghoury, *Palestine Through Sixty Years*, 3 volumes (Dar Annahar, Beirut, 1972), volume 2, 1922-1937, volume 3, 1939-1947

(3) Rafiq Farah, *A History of the Anglican Church in Jerusalem 1841-1991*, volume 2 (Jerusalem 1995) p.177

(4) Alessandro Possetto, *Il Patriarcato Latino de Gerusaleme (1848-1938)* (El Cura di Croatia, Milano, 1938) pp.567-568

(5) Ibid, p.199

(6) *The Palestinian Encyclopedia*, p.672

(7) In addition to information gathered from friends from Jerusalem, we have used the Jerusalem telephone directory of 1946 which showed more telephone number of Jews compared to telephone numbers of Arabs

(8) Emile al-Ghoury, *Palestine Through Sixty Years*, volume 2, 1922-1937, p.173

(9) Ibid, p.180

(10) *The Palestinian Encyclopedia*, pp.51-52

(11) Emile al-Ghoury, *Palestine Through Sixty Years*, volume 1, p.216

(12) Ibid, p.216

(13) All of this information is available in the booklet:
The Basic Law of the Orthodox Union Club in Jerusalem. (Jerusalem Press). The booklet was printed after the club was formed on 20 December, 1941

CHAPTER X

The Jordanian-Palestinian Union

As a result of the 1948 events, Arabs who remained in Palestinian areas that were not occupied by Jews appealed for a union with Jordan. To achieve that goal the first popular convention was held in Jericho on 1 December 1948 where a resolution was passed to unite the West Bank with the East Bank (Jordan) under the Hashemite throne. H.M King Abdullah approved the decision and the Jordanian cabinet issued a statement saying: "The Government appreciates the wish of the residents of Occupied Palestine, expressed in the Jericho Convention, as regarding a union between the two brotherly countries and will start the constitutional procedures to finalize it". On 25 December 1948 another convention was held in Nablus for all who did not participate in the Jericho convention. At its conclusion they sent a delegation to meet with King Abdullah and presented the resolutions to him. They were welcomed warmly by the King and after that the Jordanian parliament held a session in Amman, whereby a resolution was passed to agree on all resolutions of the Jericho and Nablus conventions.[(1)]

A result of those events was the start of Jordanian-Palestinian sharing in membership in cabinets, both houses of parliament and in various governmental departments and institutions. Christian participation was ever present. Anastas Hanania, the Orthodox Jerusalemite, was the first Palestinian minister from the Holy City when he became minister in the Jordanian cabinet on 12 April 1950 while other Christians started occupying their allocated seats in Parliament. Among them were: Abdullah Na'was;

Antoun Atallah; Yacoub Zayadeen;[2] Igor Farraj; Antoun Albina; Yousef Abdo; Emile Safieh; Matiyya Marroum; Emile al-Ghoury; Amin Majaj and Fouad Farraj. In the House of A'yan (Senate) Jerusalem was represented by: Anastas Hanania, Antoun Atallah and Dr Dawood Hanna. Anastas Hanania, Antoun Atallah and Fouad Farraj were appointed cabinet ministers several times. Amidst all those important events it was clear that the big developments that took place within the political arena had created a special importance for Jerusalem and its residents. The city was pushed to the front due to its global religious status. Both Arabs and Jews stuck to their points of view regarding their rights after the city was divided between them. Christians had an important role in presenting the Arab point of view since Christians in the West would be more convinced when the Arab case was presented by an Arab Christian from Arab Jerusalem where he and his ancestors lived in peaceful coexistence with Muslim Jerusalemites sharing all with them through good and bad. The developments that took place after the 1948 war, however, and the big change witnessed by Jerusalem made life more difficult for its residents. They were trying to heal their wounds and return life in Arab Jerusalem to normal when King Abdullah I was assassinated at noon on Friday, 20 July, 1951 while inside Al-Aqsa Mosque, the first *qibla* and the third mosque in Islam in terms of significance. Matters, however, improved when King Talal was proclaimed on 6 September 1951 as constitutional monarch of Jordan with his son Prince Hussein as crown prince as per article 22 of the constitution. Later, when King Talal was diagnosed as having an incurable disease, the Jordanian Crown was passed on to King Hussein on 2 May 1953. A new prosperous era started for Jerusalem and Jordan (with its two banks) with many achievements that evaporated with the 1967 war when Jerusalem was totally occupied by the Israelis.[3]

To give the reader an idea about the living conditions in Jerusalem immediately after the 1948 war I refer to a speech delivered at a Rotary club meeting by Rouhi al-Khatib who followed the city's march all his life. He was elected as member of the first municipal council (after the first Nakba of 1948) in 1951. He was chosen by the Jordanian government as the city's mayor in January 1957 and became Lord Mayor in 1959, a position he diligently served until his death. Al-Khatib mentions conditions in Jerusalem and says that Arab residents in the Arab part of the Holy City decreased from 90,000 to 33,000 while its area shrank from 12 square miles to 2.5

square miles. It suffered from shortages in electricity, water supply, hotels and financial resources, making its residents on the verge of poverty. Due to the pride and resilience of its people and their collective efforts to rebuild, the city was able to stand on its feet again. The number of hotels rose to 23 with 780 hotel rooms. Twenty-eight tourist companies were established with 18 agents for different airlines. Production and sales of handmade souvenirs improved at 68 stores in addition to a big development in the fields of travel and transport.[4]

It is only fair to give Rouhi al-Khatib his due for his devoted and dedicated service to the Arab city of Jerusalem. He spent all his life trying to fulfil his duty, as he saw it, towards the Holy City. He excelled in furthering and promoting amicable Muslim-Christian relations while paying utmost attention to the holy shrines in a manner that was internationally acknowledged. He drew praise for the friendly and hospitable manner in which the city welcomed visitors and tourists. That led to the return of its residents to the city, doubling its population to 62,000 as per the 1960 census.

During the tenure of Rouhi al-Khatib the Dome of the Rock underwent massive restoration at a cost of 700,000 Jordanian dinars from donations from the Arab and Muslim worlds.

The structure of the Church of the Holy Sepulchre was also repaired and maintained since it was damaged by the 1927 earthquake. The British Occupation Authorities supported it with iron beams which stayed all that time. Cost of repairs to the church amounted to half a million dinars covered by the three denominations that shared the arrangements of the Status Quo: Orthodox, Latins and Armenians.[5] It is unfortunate that this loyalty to the Holy City and its special status was not appreciated by the Israeli Authorities. Those authorities banished the Lord Mayor of Jerusalem on 7 March 1968 to Amman. Before that his two comrades in resisting the occupation, Sheikh Abdul Hamid al-Sayeh, Head of the Religious Appeal Court and Antoun Atallah, ex-foreign minister of Jordan, were also deported on 23 September 1967 and 22 December 1967 respectively.[6] With this, Israel started to seriously ruin Arab life in Jerusalem, pave the way to Judaize the Holy City and make the position of 'Mayor' exclusive to Zionists who work day and night to transform the city to be the unified capital of the state of Israel.

The total occupation of Jerusalem by the Israelis and their endeavours to speed up the process of changing the Muslim-Christian conditions that prevailed in the Arab part created resentment among Arab Christians towards Christians in the West who fully supported Israel without considering the feelings of Christian Arabs who are followers of churches based in the West such as the Latin church and all Protestant churches. That feeling of anger and resentment also existed among Orthodox Arabs towards the Greek monks who controlled the Orthodox Patriarchate in the Holy City. Even though the feeling of resentment among the first group did not lead, for many reasons, to any tangible actions against Western churches, the second group continued the campaign against the Greek control and against the cooperation that started between the Israeli authorities and some monks to seize Orthodox endowments that included significant portions of land and properties within the city walls and outside them. In early 1956, following the death of the Orthodox Patriarch Timotheous, leaders of the Orthodox sect called for a meeting that was held on 22 January, 1956. A preparation committee, representing all Orthodox within the patriarchate, was elected; its members were:

Representing Jerusalem: Antoun Atallah and Yousef Abdo
Representing Ramallah: Sam'an Dawood
Representing Occupied Territories: Abdallah Nusair and Raja al-Isa
Representing Gaza: Fayeq Halazoun
Representing Jordan: Sa'd Abujaber, Isa Qa'war, Sa'd
al-Nimri and Isa al-Mdanat

After deliberations, the committee added six more members to cover representation to include all areas:

Representing Bethlehem: Elias al-Bandak
Representing Nablus: Tawfiq al-Khouri
Representing Beit-Jala: Jiryes Qumsiyyah and
Ibrahim Kharoufeh
Representing Irbid: Barham Samawi
Representing Al-Karak: Farah Mdanat and
Na'im al-Qusous

The committee started its work by meeting the Jordanian Prime Minister and asking him to stop the election of the Patriarch and to hold a public convention for the Orthodox. The convention was held on 23 March, 1956 at the Orient House Hotel in Jerusalem. It was attended by Lutfi al-Mughrabi, the *Qaimmaqam* (deputy governor) of Jerusalem; Fayez Ayyoub, district commissioner of Jerusalem and his assistant Sadeq Nadheef, and 215 delegates representing all the Orthodox within the Patriarchate. Jerusalemite Antoun Atallah was elected as chairman of the convention. After lengthy deliberations it was decided to continue asking the government to confirm its wise decision to postpone holding elections for a new Patriarch to enable it to study further the Orthodox case to put matters on the right course and to end the dispute between the denomination and the Patriarchate. A decision was also taken to continue demanding the promulgation of a new legislation that would replace old laws to ensure the protection the rights of the Orthodox Arabs and fulfil their demands. Those efforts succeeded and when Suleiman al-Nabulsi`s cabinet was formed on 29 October, 1956 it started to work on a new legislation that would put an end to the dispute. Political developments, however, and the resignation of the cabinet on 10 April, 1957 delayed approving the law. It was approved later, in a strange manner, as law number 27 of 1958 in a way that did not guarantee Arabs' rights within this important Patriarchate.[7]

The Jordanian period in Jerusalem witnessed great efforts to maintain and preserve the religious character of the Holy City. Dialogue between religions was encouraged; Pope Paul VI was given a tremendous welcome during his 1964 visit, when he met with the Orthodox Patriarch Athenagoras who came especially from Constantinople, as well as with other clerics from all churches in Jerusalem. Those meetings reflected the get-together of the leaders of the Christian world after 900 years of near animosity caused by the big rift between the Church of Rome and the Church of Constantinople in AD 1054. Jordan also welcomed all heads of religions and visitors. The political situation, however, was darkening the picture after the city was divided into two parts: Arab and Jewish.

Arabs were not allowed to return to their homes, and Israel did not even allow them to visit. This forced Jordan to not allow Jews to visit Arab Jerusalem or any other part of Jordan. To those who want to delve further into this subject we refer them to a serious research paper by Dr Michel Hudson titled "Conversion of Jerusalem 1917-1988" published in the book *Jerusalem in History*.[8]

Mention has been made in previous chapters of the conflicts and disagreements that governed relations between churches in Jerusalem. One of the major conflicts was unifying festivities so that Christmas would be celebrated according to the Western Calendar while Easter would be celebrated according to the Eastern Calendar since that confirmed national feeling among Christian Arabs in general.

Responding to this general wish, a meeting was held in Amman attended by a large number of Roman Orthodox, Latins, Roman Catholics, Protestants, Copts, Assyrians (Orthodox and Catholic), Armenians (Orthodox and Catholic) and Maronites. They all supported the unifying of festivities and celebrations and formed a committee to follow up. It included Emile al-Ghoury and Emile al-Kurdi from Jerusalem plus representatives from all the above-mentioned sects.

The committee studied all aspects of the subject and consulted with Adib 'Usfour, the *Qaimmaqam* of religions in Jerusalem who was also an expert about the Status Quo. He confirmed that as for Easter, on leap years it falls on a specific day for all churches and so Eastern and Western churches can celebrate it without infringing on the rights of any, and that could be applied to all years. As for Christmas, religious rites and the Patriarchs entering the Church of Nativity could by arranged by mutual agreement if there was the will to unify celebrations".[9]

Continuous attempts were made to convince the Greek Patriarch and the Holy Synod within the Orthodox Patriarchate but all was in vain. After three years of futile attempts, Christian Arabs decided to unify Christian holidays and celebrations in Jordan starting from Christmas of 1975 and to delay matters of holidays in Palestine for the time being. Ramallah, however, decided to unify celebrations starting from 30 January, 1995 after the Arab Anglican Bishopry, headed by Bishop Sameer Qafiti took the initiative in this matter. [10]

Notes:

(1) Hani Saleem Khair, *Pictorial Historic Archives, 1920-1990* (Amman, 1991) pp.29-30

(2) Originally Dr Zayadeen was from Alsamakia village near Karak in Jordan but he served as a physician in Jerusalem and received top votes in the elections of the fifth Jordanian parliament that lasted from 1956-1961. He was however unseated due to his political stand on 12 March,1957 and was replaced by Igor Farraj

(3) Muneeb al-Madi and Suleiman Mousa, *History of Jordan in the Twentieth Century*, (Amman, 1959) p.553 onwards

(4) Read text of speech and also article about Rouhi al-Khatib in: Yacoub al-Owdat, "Thought and Literary Figures in Palestine", in Arabic, (Amman, 1976) pp.163-169

(5) Ibid, pp.163-169

(6) The list of persons deported by Israel to the East Bank between 23 September, 1967 and 6 May, 1968 amounted to ninety activists in various fields

(7) Raouf Abujaber "A Summary of the History of the Orthodox Issue" in Shehadeh and Nichola Khoury, *Summary of the History of Jerusalem's Orthodox Church*, (Amman, 1992) pp.410-414

(8) Michel Hudson, "Conversion of Jerusalem 1917-1988" in Hendricus Jacobus Franken and others, *Jerusalem in History*. English version translated by Dr Kamel Jameel al-Asali (Jordanian University, Amman, 1992)

(9) A report about the committee to unify Christian celebrations

(10) Statement of Ramallah City Published in *Church News* (Jerusalem), issues 1-3 (1995)

CHAPTER XI

The Israeli Occupation
of Arab Jerusalem

W hen Israel occupied Arab Jerusalem in June 1967 it did not hesitate to take all necessary procedures to change the status of the city and annex it to the State of Israel. It passed three resolutions that aimed, respectively, to Judaize the sovereignty, administration and the Arab Municipality. On 27 June 1967 the Israeli Knesset (Parliament) passed a resolution authorizing the government to implement the Law of Administration and Order of 1948 on any area of land the government of Israel decided to annex to the territory of Israel. On 28 June, 1967 the secretary of the government of Israel issued an order declaring that the area of Israel's territory includes the zone under the jurisdiction of Arab Jerusalem's Amana (Municipality) that falls within the sovereignty of Jordan. It is situated between the airport and Qalandia village in the north; the borders of the armistice westwards; the villages of Sour Baher and Beit Safafa in the south and the villages of Al-Tour, Isawiyya, Anata and Al-Ram in the east. The area is inhabited by 100,000 Arab residents. On 29 June, 1967 the Israel Defence Forces (IDF) issued an order to dissolve Jerusalem's Arab Municipal Council which was elected by residents of the city. The order also included ousting the Lord Mayor and merging employees of the Municipality with the municipality of the previously occupied part of the city.[(1)] Those measures in Jerusalem and in other areas of the Occupied Territories led to various activities within the corridors of the United Nations resulting in passing UN Resolution 242 on 22 November 1967 that expressed continuous worries about the dangerous and volatile situation in the Middle East. It stated that implementing the articles of the UN Charter requires having a fair and lasting peace in the Middle East, called for the withdrawal of Israeli troops from the lands occupied during the last conflict and also called for ending all war situations and for the need to work diligently for a permanent and just peace to enable every country in the region to live safely.[2]

Those significant developments, especially the complete suspension of Arab administration within the city, the deportation of Jerusalem's Lord Mayor and other leaders to Amman and the confiscation of all lands, made residents live under extreme harsh conditions that forced them to appeal to international organizations asking them to intervene to put an end to this unprecedented expansionist policy. The Muslim Council and the Christian organizations raised their voices protesting against those measures but due to harsh conditions under the Israeli Occupation activities moved to Amman where the Muslim Council delivered, on 10 September, 1970, a strong protest condemning the confiscation of land in Jerusalem. Meanwhile, Christian spiritual leaders also appealed to their superiors, on 14 September, 1970, headed by His Holiness Pope Paul VI, asking them to use their influence in the world to bring peace to the Middle East, to protect and preserve human rights within the Occupied Territories and to eliminate the injustice and calamity that befell 1,700,000 Palestinians. They also called for putting an end to the expropriation of land since Israel capitalized on current conditions and seized 12,000 dunums of land to annex them to the city of Jerusalem.[3]

In an essay by Ibrahim Matar published in 1997 and titled "The Transformation in Jerusalem", we see a clear picture of the Israeli confiscation of land that changed landmarks of life in the Holy City especially in the second phase that followed the June 1967 War and continued until the end of the century. The Israeli government used all its tools and resources to Judaize Easter Jerusalem by settling Jews in areas and properties confiscated and stolen from Palestinians and by following a racist policy that granted construction permits to Jews only, in complete and blatant violation of international law.[4]

It is important to touch on the way those events influenced the Christian presence in Jerusalem through the continuous decline in population numbers in the Holy Land, as per the detailed study by Dr Bernard Sabela;

the percentage of Christians fell from a high of 13 per cent in 1893 until it reached a low of 2 per cent of Holy Land population in 1999.[5]

This continuous decline was and still is one of the great dangers that surround the case of Arab Jerusalem and subsequently the national issue in Palestine. The causes of the emigration that resulted in the decline in number of Christians were analyzed by Palestinian researchers. Professor George Qanazi' mentioned that the emigration that is still hurting Palestinian society has many causes, mainly:

- Economic Conditions: many left, trying to find new work opportunities to better their lives. This is the same reason that makes many of them think of returning home once economic and political conditions improve.
- Political Conditions: this is a conflict that has been going on since the start of the 20th century.
- Educational: trying to pursue higher education at western educational institutes.
- Work: many leave to work in oil-producing countries.

The researcher noticed that: "The tendency to emigrate tends to be greater among the youth with unsettled futures and also more among males than females. This phenomenon, in general, has a negative social effect."[6]

The dispute between Greek clergymen within the Orthodox Patriarchate and the Orthodox Arabs within the Occupied Territories led to negative results in this respect.

Dr Saleh Hamarneh pointed to the importance of the role played by the religious endowments in putting the brakes on emigration when they are correctly managed for the benefit of the faithful reminding us of the stand of the Greek Patriarch in the Orthodox Patriarchate in Jerusalem on 22 September, 1992 when he declared: "This is our Church, this Church belongs to the Greeks; if Arabs don't accept our law then they have no alternative but choose another Church, one that they establish by themselves". This is really saddening, for when the 'Shepherd' and the 'Flock' within a church that is considered the mother of all churches are apart and feuding in the immortal city of Jerusalem, this would add to the causes of emigration and would lead to feelings of betrayal among a large number of Orthodox Christians whom Dr Bernard Sabela said came second among Christians who emigrated from Jerusalem but were first among those who return or were willing to return once conditions improve.⁽⁷⁾ As for Professor Qanazi', he also placed great importance on the role that could be played by the Orthodox Patriarchate to prevent this imminent danger.

He quoted Bishop Timotheous, Secretary of the Orthodox Patriarchate, while welcoming the convention held in Jerusalem in 2000 to discuss the problem of emigration, as saying: "Our Orthodox Church which is a local national church is invited, with sister churches in the Holy Land, to more cooperation and more devoted work to stop the haemorrhage of emigration and to more dynamism and interaction with the reality we are living. It is required, more than any other time, to play a leading role in defending justice and confronting tyranny and oppression." The writer also wondered: "Isn't it time to translate those promising words into practical, fruitful programmes?"⁽⁸⁾ Actually, he was right, for the selling of lands and properties by the monks of the Fraternity of the Holy Sepulchre frustrated Orthodox Arabs and added fuel to the ongoing dispute within the Orthodox Patriarchate.⁽⁹⁾ What saddens Orthodox Arabs is that those attempts are rather raw and aim to please Arabs in general and the Orthodox in particular who increased their protests against the Patriarchate for those violations.⁽¹⁰⁾

The above mentioned causes for emigration are repeatedly confirmed by Dr Bernard Sabela in answering the question "why do Palestinians emigrate?" He mentions that Palestinians usually emigrate because of the lack of suitable economic and career opportunities in their country. As for Christian Palestinians who, in general, belong to the middle class, they find themselves in a strange position where they are described as a "group that enjoys a high level of education and a relatively high standard of living but does not have that confidence to hope for achieving economic security or advancement and hence becomes vulnerable to this emigration." In his analysis of the circumstances of emigration in general, the researcher confirms that despite their significance they will not, seriously, change the demographic balance between Arabs and Jews for, experts unanimously confirm that the year 2015 will be the year of demographic balance. That, however, will depend on the numbers of incoming Jews arriving from different countries. Jewish estimates showed that Jewish residents in geographical Palestine would be around 6.5 million by year 2010.⁽¹¹⁾

When we discuss those important issues and their relevance to Jerusalem and to the Christian presence within it, we find it is important to mention the relations that started between the Israeli Occupation Authorities and the various Christian churches, because that gives a clear picture about the huge difference and the wide gap in thinking between Arab churches and Western churches, headed by the Vatican that enjoys having a dual character: a state on one hand and the character of a spiritual leader on the other. The dialogue between Israel and the Vatican goes back to the period before 1965 when the Second Vatican Synod absolved Jews from the blood of Jesus Christ, i.e. the removal of the accusation, that was existing at the time, that Jews killed Jesus Christ. That document was ratified by the Synod after Pope Paul VI's visit to the Holy Land in 1964. The step to ratify the document had already angered Christians in Arab countries; the Coptic Church declared its opposition to the ratification and accused Zionism of misleading the Catholic Church while Christian members of the Jordanian parliament sent a cable to the Pope denouncing the absolving of Jews from Christ's blood. Patriarch Theodosius VI (Abu Rijaileh), Patriarch of Antioch and the Orient, after a large meeting of Orthodox bishops held in Homs that week declared that "the novelty of absolving Jews from Christ's blood means the actual recognition of Israel".

All those events were accompanied by fervent Zionist activities and pressures from different circles, the most dangerous coming from the group of Cardinal Pia, the German Jesuit appointed by Pope John XXIII as Secretary of Christian Unity. He was also charged to deal with the file of Catholic-Jewish relations. All this was followed with great attention in Islamic and Christian circles due to its importance. Rouhi al-Khatib, Lord Mayor of Jerusalem, sent on behalf of the residents of the Holy City, a cable to the Pope requesting him to reconsider this important resolution since it included many dangers and provided for a perilous change of history. Other churches did not react adequately to those pressures; Greek monks decided not to interfere. Benedictus I, the Orthodox Patriarch, did not issue a protest while Belletrini, the Latin Patriarch, was an Italian national and hence could not oppose his church's stand. As for the Arab Anglican church, it was busy feuding with the English Mission about Arabizing the church and installing an Arab bishop at its head. Therefore, all activities moved to Amman where Christian Arabs sent cables of protest to the Pope via Nimah al-Sam'aan, Patriarch of Latins in Amman.

Father Ibrahim Ayyad, the well-known Palestinian patriot, travelled from Beirut to Rome where he delivered the PLO'S official protest to His Holiness, Pope Paul VI.[12]

As for the more recent dialogue between the Vatican and Israel, it started in 1992 when a bilateral committee was formed aiming to normalize relations. That was followed by signing the primary agreement on 30 December, 1993 whereby they exchanged mutual recognition and each appointed an envoy to work with the other. Both parties also undertook, as per this agreement, to combat anti-Semitism. This agreement created huge protests especially among Christians in Jordan, Syria and Lebanon. Maximus al-Sayegh Hakeem, the Roman Catholic Patriarch was the biggest protestor; on 4 June, 1994 he declared: "Our Church does not have to follow the Vatican. We are free when it comes to issues of political nature. If the Pope took a stand different from the one we currently adopt and if he erred by abandoning Jerusalem, we will strongly object to what we consider to be against our interests as Arabs".[13]

According to the primary agreement, the step that follows establishing full diplomatic relations was to form committees of experts to lay down the details of the financial and legal status of the Catholic Church and its properties in the Holy Land. Those committees had to finish their work within 24 months. It was mentioned in this respect that the Catholic Church has 300 institutes in Israel and the Occupied Territories: mainly schools, hospitals, monasteries and orphanages. Those developments accelerated the establishment of diplomatic ties between Jordan and the Vatican which was done on 3 March, 1994 whereby the Jordanian Ambassador to France was accredited as envoy to the Vatican. As for the international agreement between Israel and the Vatican, it was signed on 10 November, 1977 at the offices of the foreign ministry in West Jerusalem. Since this was accompanied by Arab protests at all levels, the Vatican issued a statement a few days later, explaining its position; it said: "the nature of this agreement is purely legal and has nothing to do with political sovereignty on lands and regions; the terrified reaction of the Palestinian Authorities was received with astonishment by the Vatican Embassy and within the Catholic Church circles. Hence this statement to explain the correct objective and meaning of this Agreement".[14] To give a clearer picture about this subject the whole Agreement is included in the addendum to this book due to its importance and role it might play in the final negotiations about Jerusalem in the future.

The Arab protest we mentioned sprang out from the public feeling that the Vatican could have postponed those steps, including exchange of ambassadors, until pending matters were solved and those included issues that resulted from the Israeli-Palestinian agreement. It was thought that the Vatican had acted singularly in trying to deal with and solve a case that concerned all Christians regardless of their sects and that it was better to have a unified Christian stand before taking such vital decisions. In addition, rushing matters like this by the Vatican harmed the Arab national cause at a time when Arabs were really appreciative of the Vatican's stands regarding their just cause throughout the years.

Here it is enough to mention only two examples of those protests. An important commentary was released by Sheikh Hasan Tahboub, the minister of endowment and religious affairs in the Palestinian Authority, published in *Al-Dustour Daily* on 13 November, 1997, vehemently condemning the agreement saying it was a dagger stabbing the peace process since the new de facto status gives Israel custody over holy shrines within the Holy City in flagrant violation of all laws and international resolutions that consider East Jerusalem an occupied territory since 1967 and therefore Israel has no right whatsoever to decide, act or act as guardian in that respect. Sheikh Tahboub also confirmed that the Palestinian Authority was taken by surprise with this agreement and hence totally rejects it and considers itself not bound by it, being an attempt by Israelis to forestall the final negotiations regarding Jerusalem.

On the Christian side, an article by Dr Raouf Abujaber, chairman of the central Orthodox Council, was published under the title of "Jerusalem needs an Arab, Muslim and Christian stand"[15] whereby he criticized the Vatican's stand and called for the urgent need: "for the quick study of the different articles of the agreement to be followed by urgent consultation with various Arab institutions connected to Jerusalem especially ministries of Endowments and Religious Affairs; Arab Muslim and Christian clergy and those in charge of Jerusalem's dossier within the Palestinian Authority (PA) and various public organizations within Jerusalem and its suburbs in order to formulate a realistic work plan and to have a unified Arab stand to face this new development". Although some contacts were made, the acceleration of events did not allow for follow-up.

One, however, must not think that the Latins Patriarchate and the custodian of the holy shrines have neglected their duties in protecting their rights and their endowments as a result of the relation that grew throughout the years between Israel and the Vatican.

One finds that relations were topsy-turvy at times and underwent legal and procedural hurdles. The best example of that is the case of the French Notre Dame Building (monastery) which was the headquarters of the Arab Jordanian Army while defending Arab Jerusalem during the 1948 war. It was sold in a fraudulent manner by an American in New York to a Jewish company owned by the Israeli National Fund. When His Holiness the Pope knew about this transaction, which was done without the Vatican's knowledge or approval, he instructed Bishop Hanna Kildani to take all necessary legal action to nullify the sale transaction. That was immediately done and at the highest level which enabled the Patriarchate to void that bogus sale and to retrieve that monastery which returned to its former status as one of the noted landmarks of Arab Jerusalem.[16]

Another example of clinging to endowments within the Latin Patriarchate is the story about the building in Arab Jerusalem near Jaffa Street. It was used by the Israelis to house the printing press of the *Jerusalem Post* daily newspaper. The Custodian of the Holy Lands, as custodian of the Terra Sancta College building (Monastery of the Franciscan Fathers), filed a suit in 1992 to evacuate the building. It finally succeeded when the case reached the Central Court. It also refused to lease out the building confirming that it would use the building for cultural, scientific and religious purposes.

This organization had previously succeeded in retrieving the well-known Terra Sancta College building in West Jerusalem when the Hebrew University, which took over the building in 1948 aided by the Israeli military, was forced to evacuate it. The college is in the same street that has the residence of Benjamin Netanyahu, the ex-prime minister of Israel.[17]

As a result of signing this agreement, Patriarch Theodorus, the current Orthodox Patriarch who is Greek, thought that it was appropriate to sign a similar one with Israel. He called for signing such an agreement and saw fit to announce this during a reception he held for Christian spiritual leaders to celebrate 1996 new year's eve. Breaking this news, the *Jerusalem Post* wrote: "After the signing of the preliminary agreement between the State of Israel and the Vatican in December 1993, it was presumed that other churches would negotiate with Israel to sign similar agreements. The Vatican, however, is the only international church which is recognized as having a sort of sovereignty that enables it to enter into treaty agreements".[18] That Israeli stand comes as no surprise for at this stage Israel wanted to control everything in Palestine, especially Jerusalem, and did not want to establish similar relations with organizations and institutions such as various churches other than the Vatican. For those, Israel created numerous and continuous difficulties via street and real estate organization plans by Jerusalem's Municipality and by levying taxes those churches cannot pay such as the Arnona and other taxes, and also through trying to seize their properties and lands whether by expropriation or purchase or long lease which happened many times with the Orthodox Patriarchate around Arab Jerusalem.[19]

Here it is important to mention an issue that preoccupied, and still does, international attention due primarily to its connection to the sponsor of the peace process and due to the influence it has in the cases of confiscating properties of 'Absentees' which Israel did immediately after the 1948 War without being accountable to anyone.

This issue or case concerns the project of building a US embassy in Jerusalem. The story started, as reported by Dr Waleed al-Khalidi in the study which was published in 2000 by the Institute of Palestinian Studies and the American Committee for Jerusalem's Affairs when Israel expanded, after the 1967 War, the boundaries covered by Arab Jerusalem Municipality from 6 square kilometres to 73 square kilometres with all the demographic change that ensued within the city. In 1970 A.I.P.A.C waged a campaign within American Congress to build the embassy in Jerusalem and continued trying until 18 January, 1987 when the US and Israel's governments signed an agreement by which the Israeli government leased to the US government a lot of land (31,250 square metres in area) for a period of 99 years, renewable, for one dollar per annum. It turned out that it was within the lands that housed the Allenby Barracks during the British Mandate. Those lands are actually owned by Al-Khalili Waqf (endowment) and is a family endowment administered and owned by Islamic Endowments and a number of Jerusalemite families, namely al-Khalidi, al-Halabi and Abu al-Seoud who had to move from Western Jerusalem due to the Israeli Occupation. on 31 May, 1989, the Arab American Atiyyah Institute headed by Michel Saba challenged this agreement and contested its legality.

Israel's seizure of Arab lands is known to all, but the endowments of the Orthodox Patriarchate were subjected particularly, continuously and successfully, to attempts by Israelis via purchasing by Israeli organizations after convincing Greek bishops who control the Patriarchate by using the method of the carrot and the stick. The deals were announced as investment deals, or long leases for periods reaching 99 years which are actually considered as sales in a country like Israel where laws and regulations are constantly changed to suit the Zionist Colonial Plan.

Those bizarre deals initiated by the Greek Patriarch and his assistants who were Greek bishops, in an illegal manner,[20] were met by strong protests by Orthodox Arab followers of the Church who vehemently opposed the deals and filed legal suits against them in various courts such as in Nazareth, Haifa, Kafr Sami', Al-Bassah, Jerusalem and Amman. The latest of those cases involved the sale of land plots 1 and 2 from basin (30297) of Mar Elias land on 18 February, 1992 with the approval of Patriarch Theodorus and with his signature. He, in an attempt to downplay and dilute the accusations that accompanied the public turmoil caused by Israel's establishing, during the tenure of Prime Minister Netanyahu, the settlement of Abu Ghonaim, the Patriarch filed a suit against the state of Israel. He authorized lawyer Mu'een Khoury, giving him a power of attorney to represent the Patriarchate in this case in front of the Israeli courts. When the court met in session on 21 March, 1997 the Israeli Ministry of Housing produced the sale deed dated 18 February, 1992 showing that the Patriarchate sold the two lots to the Municipality. The deed included "to deliver and give the right to dispose of the land, 70 dunums in area, against buyer's undertaking that it should be used for public benefit only since at the time of delivery there was no master plan for the area."[21] The judge ruled in favor of the Municipality while hitting the Patriarchy with a 2,500 shekels fine after the lawyer conceded, on 24 March, 1997, that there was an agreement signed in 1992 and therefore the case should be dropped. It is really amazing to note that such an important case took only six days since it was crucial for Israeli policy and for settlement programmes at the time that other cases took several years to be finalized.

Another important case was the one of St John's Monastery when it was occupied by force, by a Jewish extremist group called Atarot Kohnim Yesheva on 12 April, 1990. It came to the knowledge of the Lord Mayor of Jerusalem who had been deported to Amman, Mr Rouhi al-Khatib,[22] that the Patriarchate was considering an exchange deal with the Israeli Occupation Authorities whereby the Patriarchate would relinquish 750 dunums (750,000 square metres) of St John's land on the road between Jerusalem and Bethlehem in exchange for the Israelis vacating St John's Monastery within Jerusalem's old city. He wrote a memorandum to the Jordanian Prime Minister warning that if done it would pose a great danger to the Arab population in Jerusalem, Bethlehem and their surroundings.[23] The case was also discussed in *Al-Aqsa Al-Sharif* magazine, issue number 82, dated January 1992. At the same time the Palestinian Mr Michel Sindaha, who had been deported to Amman by the Israelis, published an in-depth research paper about this case.[24] The quick actions within the international media and the intervention of the Jordanian Foreign Ministry which – on 3 May, 1992 – sent an urgent letter to the Prime Minister and called the Patriarch for a meeting in Amman. This, along with other factors, led to stopping the deal. The Jewish Municipality of Jerusalem, however, later prepared new addenda to the plan through which it appropriated large areas from St John's Monastery lands.

There was also another case tied to the Patriarchate's land in Abi Toar in Jerusalem, involving the Israeli company Africania, which had been established in South Africa in 1943 by a group of Jewish investors with the objective of purchasing land for Jewish settlements in Eretz Israel. Years later it became an Israeli company with 52 per cent owned by Bank Leumi. In June 1990 this company purchased 50 per cent of the land sold by the Patriarchate to a Jewish group in 1981. This information was included in the annual report of Africania where some Orthodox activists read it, translated and published it to be read by the concerned parties.

Those cases were preceded by sales transactions in various parts of Palestine prompting many Orthodox Arabs in Palestine and Jordan to protest strongly against those illegal acts, urging authorities in both countries to preserve and protect the endowments which are closely linked to Arab heritage in Palestine, especially in Jerusalem. The Arab Orthodox Revival Society called for a convention in Amman on 8 December, 1992. It was attended by representatives of Orthodox Arabs from all parts of Palestine and Jordan. The convention received two letters of greetings and esteem from Zaid bin Shaker, the Jordanian Prime Minister, and from Yasser Arafat, head of the Palestinian Authority.

It was also attended by a large group of Jordanian and Palestinian personalities. Among them was Sheikh Abdul Hamid al-Sayeh, the official spokesman of the convention; Rouhi al-Khatib, Lord Mayor of Jerusalem; Taher al-Masri, ex-prime minister of Jordan; Abbas Zaki, member of PLO's Executive Committee; Al-Tayyeb Abdul Rahim, Palestinian Ambassador in Amman and his assistant Omar al-Khatib.

Dr Raouf Abujaber, chairman of the convention, stressed that the first message of the convention was the necessity to preserve and protect endowments and holy places. Parts of Lord Mayor of Jerusalem Rouhi al-Khatib's speech expressed accurately the general feeling among Arabs, Muslims and Christians when he said:

> As a son of Jerusalem in birth, upbringing, working and serving who spent most of his life there and later following its affairs from Amman whenever I passed through Ephtymus Market in the middle of the old city known as Dabbagha (Tanners) market and whenever I had the pleasure of spending school outings in Galalia land in the Mount of Olives and in the lands of Al-Shayyah Monastery near Gethsemane and the lands of Qatamoun and Musallaba Monasteries or the lands of Mar Elias Monastery between Jerusalem and Bethlehem all property of the distinguished sect I couldn't but appreciate and admire the efforts of those in charge who acquired and preserved those valuable properties and assets.
>
> My respect and esteem for the men of this sect grew after I became Mayor of the city and later its Lord Mayor (Ameen), after I contacted them and viewed, first hand, more and more of its properties and its religious and real-estate institutions in Jerusalem and its surroundings. Those included a number of churches, monasteries and schools including the building of the Municipality within the old city, the Patriarchate complex, St John's Hostel, St Mark's Hotel (leased by the Dajani family and which faces Jerusalem's Citadel) and other beautiful residential buildings around the Church of the Holy Sepulchre.
>
> All that appreciation and esteem became mingled with worry and grief when I later heard about deals that sold large tracts of land owned by the sect in and around Jerusalem; deals that were finalized between those in charge of the sect and the Israeli Occupation Authorities. Those deals included the land on which the Israeli Knesset is built in Jerusalem, and which was originally the sect's land part of Al-Musallaba Monastery. My worry and grief increased lately when I received the

troubling news about other deals concerning the sect's properties in Jerusalem and Jaffa, the most important of which are the cases of St John's Hostel in Jerusalem and the lands of Mar Elias Monastery between Jerusalem and Bethlehem and the land of the cemetery in Jaffa. [25]

The great concern that overtook Arab Jerusalem's Society over the sale of lands and the huge dispute that grew between Orthodox Arabs and their institutions on one side and the Patriarch and his Greek monks and aides led the Jordanian government to intervene at the highest levels especially since it was responsible for issuing law number 27 for the year of 1958 named Law of Jerusalem's Roman Orthodox Patriarchate. It tried to ensure the continuity of Jordanian jurisdiction over the holy sites in Jerusalem as per agreements signed after Israel's occupation of Jerusalem in 1967. The Palestinian Authority also became engrossed by this issue especially since it was trying to strengthen its foothold in Jerusalem after signing the Oslo Accords. Therefore it was only natural to find that the signing of the Agreement by Israel and the Vatican towards the end of 1997 created waves of anger among the circles of the Palestinian Authority and among Palestinians, especially Christians who always demanded that the Vatican take a more balanced stand that took the side of justice and truth in the Palestinian- Israeli struggle. Hence, the Palestinian Authority in early 1998 started contacts with the Vatican followed by negotiations that lasted nearly two years. The Palestinian Authority was represented by an official delegation that included Christian Palestinians headed by Dr Emile Jarjooi, a member of the executive committee of the PLO. Its member included Mitri Abu Ayta, minister of tourism; Nabeel Qassees, minister in charge of the Bethlehem 2000 Project and Mr Hanna Naser, Mayor of Bethlehem. Those negotiations resulted in signing what was called "an historic agreement " since it gave the existence of the Catholic Church within Palestinian lands an official stamp. The agreement was signed at the Vatican on Tuesday, 15 February 2000 by His Holiness Pope John Paul II and Palestinian President Yasser Arafat. The most important of its contents was the call for a fair and just solution for Jerusalem and giving it a special status with international guarantees to preserve its special identity and its holy stature.

The Agreement stresses freedom of religion and thought and the equality between the three heavenly religions and for free access to the holy places.

The reader will find the full text of this agreement in the addendum published at the end of this book.[26]

All those events occurred at the time when the Palestinian problem underwent stages of the peace process that followed the Gulf War of 1991. The Madrid Peace Convention started on 30 October of that year, followed by the bilateral talks on 3 November and by the mutual recognition between Israel and the PLO on 9 and 10 September 1993 and the signing of the Oslo 1 Accords by Itzhak Rabin and Yasser Arafat in Cairo on 13 September 1993, and finally the peace treaty between Jordan and Israel was signed on 26 October 1994. The peace process, however, stumbled when the right-wing coalition, led by Netanyahu won the elections of 29 May 1996, decided to open the tunnel in Jerusalem on 27 September 1997 and established the 'Abu Ghonaim Mountain Settlement on 25 February 1997. When Ehud Barak, the Labour candidate, won on 17 May 1999 matters were already out of hand; the whole case was rerouted towards total confrontation and towards the Al-Aqsa Intifada at the end of 2000.

During those years the residents of Arab Jerusalem found themselves in extremely difficult situations; those circumstances prevented them from any activities: their lives were only concerned with protecting the holy places and in trying to stop Zionist colonial expansion that aimed to expropriate the largest possible areas of Arab land. Arab churches felt the danger and tried their best to direct public opinion, local and international, to the danger posed by the Israeli attack especially in Jerusalem. The protests of Arab spiritual leaders acted as alarm bells trying to defend the holy shrines and the Arab identity of Jerusalem.

Along with those Arab stands, there were regional and international clerical initiatives to confirm that Occupied Arab Jerusalem was still Arab and that matters should go back to pre-June-1967 status while adhering to United Nations resolutions and greatly attending to the holy shrines and ensuring freedom of access to them.[27] At the same time the Vatican announced its desire to participate in the negotiations about the future of Jerusalem when its foreign minister, Bishop Jean Louis Touran declared on 26 October 1998 that:

> Jerusalem has too high a status of holiness to have its fate decided by Palestinians and Israelis only. The Vatican believes in the importance of expanding representation at the

negotiations table to make sure that none of the issues are bypassed and to confirm that the whole international community is responsible for the holiness and sanctity of the unique city. Therefore it is important that all parties take into consideration, properly and justly, the international and holy stature of the city.[28]

As for Greece's head cleric, Christo Dolu – Archbishop of Athens and All Greece, he declared on 26 August 2000 during his visit to Bethlehem that: "Any agreement should respect the three religions: Christianity, Judaism and Islam, and it is essential that Palestinians should retrieve their rights."[29]

In this respect it is important to explain the Jordanian position regarding the issue of Arab Jerusalem, which, along with the West Bank, was under Jordan's jurisdiction between the years of 1948 and 1967 and to whom Jordan felt responsible for its holy places. Due to the importance of this subject we find it prudent to mention what was announced by Jordan about its responsibility towards waqfs (endowments) and holy shrines in Jerusalem, as mentioned in the book issued by the government titled: *The Peace Agreement between The Hashemite Kingdom of Jordan and the State of Israel on 26 October 1994*. Following is a part of its text:

> Responsibility towards endowments and holy shrines in Jerusalem is a holy responsibility carried by the Hashemites since 1924 out of their conviction that they should protect Islamic shrines in Palestine. Hajj Amin al-Husseini, head of the supreme Islamic Council has requested Prince Abdallah Ibn al-Hussein on 30 August 1924 to have the entire area of Al-Haram al-Sharif in Jerusalem under his patronage. This patronage continued until this day. When Jordan dismantled the administrative and legal ties with the West Bank, turning them over to the PLO, that did not include endowments and holy places confirming Jordan's insistence on protecting, serving and maintaining them as also was requested by the Palestinian side.
>
> It was agreed by the Palestinian party and Israel to defer discussing the final status of the city of Jerusalem until year 1996 as per clause 3 of article 5 of the Palestinian-Israeli principles agreement signed on 13 September 1993."

Jordan undertook that when Palestinians and Israelis reach agreement on the final and permanent status of Jerusalem to transfer the custody of endowments and holy sites from Jordanian to Palestinian custodianship.

What was stated in the Jordanian-Israeli Agreement and Washington's announcement that Israel respects the special, current role played by the Hashemite Kingdom of Jordan towards Islamic holy places in the city of Jerusalem is a clear recognition of an historic mission carried out by the Hashemites from 1924 until now. Jordan, in its agreements with Israel, insisted on protecting Palestinians' rights in the Holy City which is considered among the territories occupied in June 1967. Article (B) of the work agenda of negotiations in the Jordanian – Israeli agreement signed on 14 September 1993 and under article 5 (Borders and land issues) we find the following:

> settlement of land issues and assigning agreed upon border markers for the international borders between Jordan and Israel by going back to border definition under the British Mandate without harming the status of any of the lands that became under Israeli military control in 1967.
>
> Thus Jordan preserved sovereignty in the West Bank relinquishing it only to the Palestinian side and not to Israel and also prevented the transfer of responsibility for Islamic Holy Places within the Holy City to the Israeli Ministry of Religions.[30]

It is very obvious that the Palestinian Authority, despite its desire to hold all the reins when it comes to affairs dealing with Palestinian existence, yet found it prudent to accept this arrangement imposed by facts on the ground considering its shaky relations with Israel. The PA, however, was doing all it could to confirm and strengthen Palestinian rights over the holy places. President Yasser Arafat persisted in attending Christmas ceremonies within the Church of Nativity in Bethlehem every year to confirm those rights. He also made a very important decision by which the PA handed to the Russian Orthodox Church some properties it owned in the Bethlehem area which were seized earlier by secessionist clergymen following the Bolshevik

Revolution of 1917 and who were based in New York calling themselves the White Russian Church.[31]

President Arafat also welcomed the delegation of the Central Orthodox Council headed by its chairman, Dr Raouf Abujaber with more than twenty Orthodox dignitaries from Jordan and Palestine on early Thursday, 22 May 1997. President Arafat promised them to do his best to settle the dispute between Orthodox Arabs and the Greek Patriarch and monks in Jerusalem. He also added that he would strongly oppose any illegal action regarding the endowments.

Although talk usually centred most of the time on responsibility towards Islamic endowments, Jordanian guardianship was also requested by Christians as shown by the continued validity of Jordanian law number 27 of 1958 and by Jordan's explicit interest in whatever affected Christian affairs. King Hussein of Jordan wrote to Patriarch Theodorus on 13 August 1994 saying

> We received with thanks and appreciation your kind letter carrying your greetings from Holy Jerusalem, the place the faithful yearn to see and by which you expressed your strong faith in our Hashemite leadership and your full support of our endeavours to achieve a just and permanent peace that will satisfy future generations and whom the Washington Declaration was one of its main stages. We like to confirm, here that the Jordanian Hashemite role in protecting Islamic and Christian Holy Sites in Jerusalem will continue, with God's permission, as we always did in protecting and defending them. Sovereignty over them is for God (Allah) only while guardianship is a legal right of the nation. At the moment when we stick to our religious and legal Hashemite role, which will never be interrupted, yet we will get inspiration from the "Covenant of Omar" which you stressed, in your letter, the degree to which it represents sublime meanings and exalted Islamic Values.

This letter was preceded by an important statement by King Hussein during his address to the Foreign Relations Committee in the Jordanian senate on 13 February 1994 in Amman. It was published in toto in *Al-Dustour Daily* on 14 February 1994.

A few years later Prince Hassan, Jordan's crown prince at the time, played an active role in the dispute that erupted between the Department of Islamic Endowments in Jerusalem and the Orthodox Patriarchate regarding Al-Khanqah (Salahiyya). The dispute was over property borders between the Islamic waqfs (endowments) on one side and the Roman Orthodox Patriarch, the Armenian Orthodox Patriarch and the custodian of the holy sites on the other side. When the dispute intensified, the three sent a letter dated April 1497 to Prince Hassan "explaining to HRH the circumstances of the unjust assault that targeted the roof of the Church of the Holy Sepulchre, at the spot between the Church and Saladin Mosque where toilets were built and the wall of two rooms within a house inside the Roman Orthodox Patriarchate was demolished. They asked the prince to participate in solving the problem to put a stop to those who want to damage the brotherly relations that bind the residents of the Holy City; it would also stop foreign elements that try to capitalize on this unfortunate event." Here they are referring to Israel's continuous attempts to intervene in the dispute by adding oil to the fire between Muslims and Christians in Jerusalem.

Ten days later Engineer Adnan al-Husseini, Director of Waqfs (endowments) in Jerusalem sent a letter along with a detailed report about the case to the Minister of Waqfs and Islamic Affairs in Amman dated 24 April 1997. In it he mentioned that there is escalation or development in the case, after it was thought to be contained, through the Israeli attempts to intervene helped by certain parties – by escalating the incident in the media. He complained about the Orthodox Patriarchate which had agreed before on the formation of a technical committee to study the conflicting views between the Islamic Restoration Committee and the Patriarchate. Now he complains the Patriarchate retracted. Therefore he requested work to be stopped until circumstances change and until solutions, preserving rights of both parties, are reached.

Immediately, Prince Hassan formed a committee consisting of Dr Kamel Abujaber; Dr Hazem Nusseibeh and Engineer Ra'ef Najm, all ex-cabinet ministers, and Dr Kamel Hamarneh. The committee visited the Holy City and met with the conflicting parties and submitted its report to the prince on 19 June 1997 through the Minister of Waqf and Islamic Affairs. The report said

> The Orthodox Patriarch assured us that it is vital not to allow
> any Israeli party to interfere in the matter which we consider

to be a simple dispute between brothers and should be kept within the same family. He praised the brotherly relations between Christians and Muslims who lived together amicably and peacefully since the 'Omar Covenant' and through the Hashemite Jordanian era. The Patriarch does not want to shake this relationship; he is trying to strengthen it. He is sadly affected, however, by the method used by the Restoration Committee in tearing down the wall and by the assault on the sanctity of the place and by dumping the monk's clothes outside.

The dispute was considered over when the head and members of the Islamic Waqfs Council paid a visit to the Patriarch. Pleasantries were exchanged and the council submitted a written undertaking not to allow any future encroachment on Christian properties in Jerusalem. It was agreed to leave matters in Al-Khanqah (Salahiyya) as they are now.[32]

On 10 August 1998 Prince Hassan formed a fact-finding panel consisting of Dr Kamel Abujaber, Dr Hazem Nusseibehh and Engineer Ra'ef Najm – Dr Kamel Hamarneh with the participation of Michel Hamarneh "to find a solution for the ongoing dispute about the Patriarchate's lands within the West Bank and Israel and also to remove the tension between Arab followers of the Orthodox Faith in Jordan and Palestine and between the Patriarch and the Fraternity of the Holy Sepulchre". The Committee visited Jerusalem on 20 November 1998 and submitted its preliminary report to Prince Hassan on 2 January 1999 in which it confirmed that the Patriarch had agreed to activate law number 27 of 1958 and that properties in various locations were leased for 99-year periods and that it needed to pay more due diligence to the lands especially since the promise made by Bishop Timotheous, secretary of the Patriarchate, to supply copies of the agreements between the Patriarchate and the lessee companies was not fulfilled. The Committee ended by saying that "it stressed in its talks with the Patriarch and his assistants the importance of openness, transparency and active participation of the flock in the process of decision making especially when it comes to the properties of the Orthodox Church." The Committee also requested the Patriarchate "not to sign any agreements in the future with any investment companies before consulting with Jordan". Those wishes expressed by the Committee stayed as wishes; there was no transparency and no active participation by the flock and Jordan was never consulted regarding any investment deals which were in reality the illegal sale of Orthodox endowments.

The Jordanian position concerning the guardianship over the Holy Sites remained as we mentioned. On 10 November 1999 the Jordanian Prime Minister, Abdul Raouf al-Rawabdeh, denied that the Hashemite Kingdom of Jordan "had stopped administering the holy sites in Jerusalem" stressing that it did not decide that. He also stressed that Jordan had looked after those sites and protected them from reaching the hands of the Israeli Ministry of Religion. He added that "until our Palestinian brothers will be able to carry on the responsibility of administering the Holy Sites and protecting them from falling into the hands of the Israeli Ministry of Religion, Jordan will be ready to do that, for we have no intention of interfering in the matters of the coming Palestinian State but will be backers and supporters of that State, and this is what we made very clear to our brothers."[(33)]

To describe fully the details of this important issue the author finds it imperative to note the special interview published in *Al-Dustour Daily* on 6 September, 2000 in Amman with Pope Shenouda III, Pope of Alexandria and Patriarch of St Marcus Karaza. He stated that the issue of Jerusalem is a very complex subject and one of the most difficult in the negotiations since the Jews cling to Jerusalem as their religious centre and the Palestinians insist that it is the capital of their state.

Commenting on various proposals regarding Jerusalem, Pope Shenouda, in his interview with the BBC, said that leaving the sovereignty over the city "to God" was a vague proposal. He also said that leaving Jerusalem under international rule meant Arabs relinquishing the city and leaving it to other states where it could lead to Jewish sovereignty. Pope Shenouda said there is a difference between worship and sovereignty: worship is guaranteed for all; as for sovereignty, it is a political matter.

Arab Christianity and Jerusalem

Notes:

(1) Rouhi al-Khatib, *The Judaization of Jerusalem*, (Amman, 1970), part 1, p.12

(2) War of 1967 in the UN Organization, *The Palestinian Encyclopedia*, 2 parts in 10 volumes. (Damascus, 1948-1990) p.184

(3) Rouhi al-Khatib, *The Judaization of Jerusalem*, pp.101-105

(4) Ibrahim Matar, *The Transformation of Jerusalem 1948-1997*, (London, 1997), p.14

(5) Bernard Sabela's study "Palestine Christians and Future Tasks" published among a series of articles December 1999 under the supervision of Afif Safieh, Palestinian Ambassador to UK, p.15

(6) George Qanazi' Paper presented to the Orthodox Convention in Jerusalem, June 2000, published in Al-Sunnarah, 4 August 2001

(7) Saleh Hamarneh, "Role of Endowments in the steadfastness of Jerusalem and the position of the Orthodox Patriarchate". A paper presented to: The Ninth Seminar on Jerusalem's Day, p. 151

(8) George Qanazi's Paper on Immgration, in Liqa' Centre in Jerusalem, 1991.

(9) *Al-Sunnara*, issue dated August 4, 2001. Supplement, page (7)

(10) This big dispute between Orthodox Arabs who total, within the Jerusalem Orthodox Patriarchate, around 200,000 persons in Jordan and Palestine and the Greek monks of the Fraternity of the Holy Sepulchre who number 90 only, including the Patriarch, bishops and monks and who have absolute control over the Patriarchates affairs, it goes back to Ottoman times when the "Milla Nizam" allowed them to infiltrate and occupy leading positions within the Patriarchate. Result is that until now there is no Arab bishop, in flagrant violation of customs, traditions and articles of Jordanian law number 27 of 1958 that explains the legal matters of this Patriarchate and which stipulated Arab-Greek partnership in managing and supervising endowments and shrines.

(11) *Christians in the Holy Land* (conference), edited by Michel Prior and William Taylor (London, Institute of Islamic Culture, 1994), p.44

(12) The Vatican, in *The Palestinian Encyclopaedia*, volume 3, pp.417-421

(13) Interview with the Roman Catholic Patriarch Maximus V Hakeem in *Al-Safeer Daily* (Lebanon), issue of 4 June, 1994

(14) This statement, with a copy of the Agreement were presented to me by the late Monsignior Raouf al-Najjar who worked for a long period as acting envoy at the Apostolic Mission in Amman.

(15) Raouf Abu Jaber, "Jerusalem needs and Arab, Muslim and Christian stand", *Al-Rai Daily*, Amman

(16) Rouhi al-Khatib, *The Judaization of Jerusalem*, volume 2, p.72

(17) *Jerusalem Post*, 31 December 1995

(18) *Al-Rai Daily*, Amman, 19 November 1998

(19) The *Arnona* is a municipal tax levied on properties (similar to the Musakkafat tax in Jordan) in return of municipal rendered services. Israel strictly enforces it on Arabs in accordance with its settlements policies. In some cases this tax reaches 25 percent of the revenue of the property.

(20) Those issues were the main reasons for the chronic dispute between the Patriarch and the Fraternity of the Holy Sepulchre within the Jerusalem Orthodox Patriarchate on one hand and the Orthodox Arabs who followed the Patriarchate in Jordan and Palestine on the other hand.

(21) Photocopies of this deal and its related documents were published in *Annahar Daily*, Beirut, September 13, 1997, p.1

(22) News of this deal reached the Mayor of Arab Jerusalem through a call from Mr Louis Katan in Paris. He is the son of Henry Katan, the faithful son of Jerusalem and read about the deal in the *Kol Heimer Paper* published in Israel on 3 April, 1992

(23) Letter of the office of Jerusalem Municipality to H.E The P.M in Amman No. 5/33 dated 11 April, 1992 and signed by the Mayor of Arab Jerusalem, the late Mr Rouhi al-Khatib

(24) Mr Michel Sindaha kindly supplied me with a copy of his valued research titled: *The Judaization of the Christian Quarter in Jerusalem collides with the rock of Muslim-Christian solidarity: the story of the occupation of the Hostel – St. John's Monastery in Jerusalem*

(25) Part of the speech delivered by the late Rouhi al-Khatib, Lord Mayor of Jerusalem, in the opening session of the fifth Orthodox convention held in Amman on 8 December, 1992 which I chaired in my capacity as chairman of the Arab Orthodox Revival Society that called for and organized the convention

(26) Dr Emile Jarjoui was kind enough to supply me with a copy of the agreement.

(27) Examples of those initiatives are in Bishop Samir Qafiti's lecture in Rabat, Morocco in October 1993 and also in the lecture delivered by the late Faisal al-Husseini at the Institute of Unified Forces for Defense studies, London during May, 1996

(28) Statements of H.H The Pope in *Al-Rai Daily* 23 March, 2000; *Al-Dustour Daily*, 19 September, 2000

(29) Statements Published in *Al-Dustour Daily*, 26 August, 2000

(30) The Jordanian Media Committee, *Peace Agreement Between Hashemite Kingdom of Jordan and Israel*, 26 October, 1994 (Amman: The committee, 1994

(31) As quoted in *Al-Rai Daily*, Amman, 17 January, 2000

(32) Work documents of both committees. Presented to me by Dr Kamel Hamarneh

(33) As per statements published in *Al-Rai Daily*, Amman, 11 November, 1999

CHAPTER XII

The Role of Jerusalem in Resisting
the Israeli Occupation

One has to agree that the last decade of the 20th century was of great significance to the Palestinian issue in general and to Jerusalem's case in particular. At its onset the first intifada stopped and the Gulf War occurred, while its end witnessed the start of the second intifada (the Al-Aqsa Intifada) which became the symbol of the Palestinian stand after everyone lost confidence in the peace process. Apparently that loss of confidence was completely directed at the US stand which was supposed to play the role of honest broker between the Israelis and the Palestinians, which did not happen, creating resentment throughout the Arab world. This resentment dominated the feelings of Arab Christian clergy within Jerusalem's churches in particular as a result of their existence on the battlefield and their consciousness about the pains and sufferings of the city's residents that lasted for many years interspersed with short periods when they felt hope of arriving at a just solution that would give them back their rights and protect the sanctity of Jerusalem and its role as a safe haven for all believers without discrimination.

It is our duty, therefore, to give an idea about national activity within the four Arab churches in Jerusalem: the Orthodox Patriarchate; the Latin Patriarchate; the Anglican Bishopry and the Roman Catholic Bishopry. In the first, Patriarch Theodorus I was elected to the post of Patriarch for the Holy City of Jerusalem for the Roman Orthodox on 16 February, 1981 according to Jordanian law after fierce elections between three candidates amidst strong opposition from a large number of Orthodox Arabs who asked the Jordanian government to activate the articles of Jordanian law number 27 of 1958 to fix the financial and administrative flaws, to pay more attention to the flock's affairs and to put an end to the illegal disposal of endowments and properties. Since the Jordanian government supported the election of Patriarch Theodorus, after he promised to introduce reform, this royal decree was issued recognizing his election using the following text:

> For what we know of his loyalty to us and to the Hashemite Dynasty and for his tact, ability and knowledge in managing spiritual affairs and ensuring love and equality among the Roman Orthodox Sect members we declare our recognition and endorsement of this election. We express our Royal agreement to the appointment of His Eminence Theodorus I to this position and forward to him all the above stated powers and rights and enable him to use them. We bestow on him all the rights and privileges attached to this position according to the law and according to traditions and conventions.[1]

The Patriarchate's body in that year consisted of the Patriarch and seventeen bishops and priests who were members of the Holy Synod in addition to eighty-six bishops, priests and deacons who were members of the Fraternity of the Holy Sepulchre. All were Greeks with the exception of two Arabs.[2]

Before his election, the Patriarch made many promises publicized by a statement, read in his presence in front of a large audience by one of the priests at Al-Abdali Church in Amman on 16 February 1981. None of those promises was fulfilled, as was customary with the Fraternity of Holy Sepulchre who always declared that the Orthodox Patriarchate is a Greek institution and that no one has the right to interfere in its affairs. That contradicts the contents of the above mentioned statement by the Patriarch where he discussed his efforts to serve while he was the Patriarchate's Bishop in Amman and how he confronted the rigid stand of the late Patriarch, Benedictus, and his loyal men.[3] After he assumed office he started a plan, helped by some Greek monks, to collect funds by pressuring Orthodox families residing in the Patriarchate's properties to vacate them. The plan also included the sale and long-lease of lands and properties in blatant violation of his responsibilities as Patriarch of the oldest church in Jerusalem and those stands and attitudes led to strong conflicts between him and the Greek monks within the Patriarchate on one side and Orthodox Arabs in Jordan and Palestine on the other. Those conflicts were some of the reasons that drove a number of Orthodox families and their youth to emigrate. There was, however, another reason for the conflict which was the Patriarchate's refraining from playing any role to defend the rights of Arabs who were suffering under the occupation. Not a single statement by the Patriarch or any of his aides that could be interpreted as anti-Israeli was issued, thus protecting the dubious relation between both parties. In addition to keeping this post until his death on 19 January, 2000, he toiled all his life to win the favour of the Jordanian and Palestinian Authorities, and co-signed once in a while collective statements initiated by other churches such as the statement issued by nine churches on 14 January, 1992 denouncing the Occupation's destruction of monasteries and ancient ruins and calling for protection for the holy shrines in Jerusalem. This statement was also signed by the Latin Patriarch, the Armenian Patriarch, the Anglican Bishop, the Lutheran Bishop, the Roman Catholic Deputy Patriarch, the heads of the Franciscan Order charged with protecting the Holy Sites, the Assyrian Bishop and the Bishop of the Copts.[4] This deafening silence from the Patriarch and the Greek monks continued until 1998 when an Arab voice rose from within the walls of the Patriarchate: that of Archmenderit Atallah Hanna, the official spokesman of the Orthodox Church in Jerusalem and the Holy Land. He started a campaign to protect the holy shrines and to preserve Arabs' rights using conferences, seminars, the press and TV channels. This made up for some of the losses incurred by the Patriarchate's period of silence since the Occupation started.[5]

This loud voice calling for right and justice annoyed the Israeli Authorities to the extent that the Israeli Ministry of Religions sent a letter to the Patriarch dated 3 May, 2000 protesting statements made by Archmenderit Atallah Hanna and saying

"he calls himself the official spokesman of the Orthodox Church within the Holy land… we do not recognize this job title which does not conform with the Greek Orthodox Patriarchate. He also called on all the churches in the world to support the Palestinian National Struggle and its national aspirations that include regaining Palestinian rights, retrieval of the Occupied Territories and confirming Palestinians' right of return and establishing a Palestinian State with Jerusalem as its capital. He stressed that the present conditions will bring about an explosion. We look at those statements made by Arch-menderit Atallah Hanna on behalf of the Greek Orthodox Patriarchate very seriously because of the extremely negative tone he uses in attacking the State of Israel and its policies, and more so because of the blatant interference of a clergyman within the Patriarchate in political issues that are not within his jurisdiction. We advise your Eminence that if you do not take the necessary disciplinary measures against this Archmenderit who claims that he speaks for the Patriarchate then we reserve the right to review the whole relationship we have with the Greek Patriarchate in Jerusalem.[6]

The letter caused anxiety among the Greek monks but the Patriarch's illness and his worry about anticipated angry reaction by Palestinians and other Arabs made him slow down so he did not take any action. The Archmenderit carried on his work and statements, the strongest of which was a statement he made six months after the Patriarch's death on 1 July 2001 when he said "there will be no bargaining and no compromise to relinquish even one grain of the soil of the Occupied Arab Jerusalem, for Jerusalem was and will be Arab forever and it should return under Arab sovereignty as the capital of the independent State of Palestine." He also directed attention to the loss of the freedom to worship and denounced the continuation of the Israeli occupation saying: "sooner or later Jerusalem will return to us. It is for Arabs alone; they are the ones who protected its shrines and guaranteed freedom of worship within it and access to reach the Holy Shrines. They guaranteed the followers of all religions the freedom to practise their rituals and worship. All this changed when the Israelis occupied Jerusalem: now there is no freedom of worship and no freedom to move and reach the holy sites. Muslims and Christians are deprived of reaching the Church of the Holy Sepulchre and Al-Aqsa Mosque."[7]

Unfortunately, all those genuine efforts by Archmenderit Atallah Hanna could not stop the illegal disposal of Orthodox endowments and properties while no information is divulged by the Patriarchate since the monks, headed by the Patriarch, cloak these dealings with utmost secrecy. International media, however, manages sometimes to dig up some facts and present them to public opinion that can only protest due to conditions under the Occupation. An example is the news item published in the London daily, *Al-Hayat*[8] about the Patriarchate leasing a 527-dunum lot of land to Israel "forever". That is a new type of leasing since previous leases were for a period of 99 years. In addition, *Ma'ariv Daily*[9] published an article about investigations by the Israeli International Crimes division that showed that the amount paid by the Jewish National Fund (16 million dollars) was found in a secret bank account in Switzerland and "the local party that deposited it declared that it was in the name of the Greek Patriarch. The police are investigating if the amount was deposited by Jacob Rabinovitch or by his son Zcisman who both acted as middlemen in the deal between the Patriarch and the Jewish National Fund since the Patriarch did not receive the funds as he claimed in his complaint to the Israeli Police."

As for the Latin Patriarchate, it enjoys a good discipline and feels very strongly about holding on to its endowments. National activities within the Patriarchate started in the nineties when the Pope, on 6 January, 1988, selected the Arab clergyman Michel Sabbah (from Nazareth) to be the Latins Patriarch for the Holy City. His reign started in an Arab atmosphere not seen by the Patriarch since its establishment in 1847 when all its Patriarchs were Italian.

Considering the suffering of Arab Palestinians under the Occupation the new Patriarch did not hesitate to call for freedom and justice for them. In a statement issued by the heads of the Christian sects in Jerusalem he denounced and condemned the Haram Al-Sharif Massacre of 8 October, 1990 and the creation of an atmosphere of provocation that leads to struggle and confrontation.

On 10 August 1992 he, along with Sheikh Sa'd al-Din Alalami, Mufti of Jerusalem; Sheikh Mohammad Hussein, Imam of Al-Aqsa Mosque; Bishop Lutfi Laham, the Roman Catholic Prelate 3 and Bishop Sameer Qafiti, Prelate of the Anglican Church, sent a letter to the Vatican on behalf of Muslims and Christians who had been in Palestine since 1948 asking that their just cause not be forgotten and asking for the non-adoption of any policy that might jeopardize the status of the Holy City in the future. [10] From the day he became the head of the Latin Church, Patriarch Sabbah warmly and faithfully defended Arab existence in Jerusalem and Palestine through his numerous sermons and through his various statements to the press and other media. To give an idea about the comprehensiveness of those efforts we mention here some of the information that reached us. The heads of the Christian Sects issued a second statement on 24 December 1992 that considered eviction and collective deportation of Palestinians as a form of collective punishment that is unacceptable and called to the people to hold on to their lands.

On 11 April 1993 and on the occasion of Easter the Patriarch declared "enough violence, enough blood and enough injustice and discrimination between the Israeli and Palestinian people". On the same occasion on 16 April, 1995 he shouted that the message of Easter is "Hope and Wishes" and that coveted peace could only be attained by real reconciliation in Jerusalem. On the occasion of Christmas, in Bethlehem, he criticized Israel for freezing the peace process. He also condemned the American-Anglo strikes against Iraq.[11] While visiting Al-Dehaishah Refugee Camp he stated that when he arrived at Beit Jala from Nazareth he became a refugee and the right of the refugee is derived from God and should not be abandoned and that no force on earth can seize man's right in his country and land.

He also called for building a new, distinctive Arab Palestinian state for after a hundred years of sacrifices and bloodshed we cannot return as a state like other states.[12] In his Christmas sermon the Patriarch said that peace with the Palestinian people is the core of the issue and the main prerequisite for having peace in the region, pointing at the same time to the fact that peace in our Holy Land is a tough march full of hurdles. He also called for justice and freedom for all Palestinian prisoners of war and refugees.[13].

As for the Al-Aqsa Intifada he considered it a quest for a free and dignified life within an independent Palestinian state with Jerusalem as its capital. This he voiced while performing Sunday mass within the Church of Nativity in Bethlehem which was followed by a special prayer for the souls of martyrs who died for the cause. That was followed by a demonstration where more than two thousand Muslims and Christians chanted "side by side, Muslims and Christians until liberation".[14] During Christmas celebrations, Patriarch Sabbah called for a just solution for the Holy City and asked the Occupation Authority to put an end to preventing the faithful from reaching their places of worship. Palestinians, he said, should by given whatever is Palestinian in Jerusalem.[15] During midnight mass he called for an end to Palestinians' suffering and for realizing justice and freedom for the Palestinian people. Christian celebrations, as decided by all Christian churches, were restricted to performing religious rites only.[16]

Naturally, all those statements annoyed the Israeli Authorities who never approved of the sermons made by Patriarch Sabbah or other Arab clergymen. In a special press conference, Yuri Mor, director of the Department of Christian Sects within the Israeli Ministry of Religions, accused Patriarch Sabbah of inciting trouble saying that 99 per cent of the Latin Patriarch's mission was political and advised the Patriarch to stay only as a religious leader.[17] Israel voiced, on many occasions, its dissatisfaction with those statements by closing the roads in the face of the Patriarch's procession during many of his visits to various churches.

While discussing the activities of the Latin Patriarchate in Jerusalem it is noteworthy to mention its big accomplishment in realizing two historical Papal visits to Palestine and Jordan with complete success and without a hitch. In addition to the visit made by Pope Paul VI in early 1964 during which he met Athenagoras, the Orthodox Patriarch of Constantinople, in Jerusalem and other Patriarchs within the Holy City, and, received by King Hussein bin Talal, Pope John Paul II made a visit on 20 March, 2000 where he was welcomed and received by King Abdallah II of Jordan and by Yasser Arafat. Those visits were very significant and had a positive impact on the world in general and on the Catholic world in particular, for to Catholics Papal visits are considered laden with holiness and human compassion that strengthen love and brotherhood among people. Visits also encourage large numbers of the faithful to follow in the Pope's footsteps, especially his visit to Bethany (the site where Jesus' baptism was performed) which was followed by a visit on the East Bank of the River Jordan.

In the years following his visit, Pope Paul VI voiced his worry about the growing decrease in the number of Christians within the Holy City. He expressed those worries in his Papal message issued on the occasion of Easter in 1974 when he said: "Those brothers and sisters who are living where Christ has lived and who are still around the holy places, they are the successors of the first church. They are the origin of all churches and if Christian presence is eliminated from Jerusalem then the fire of live testimony in the Holy Land will be extinguished and holy shrines in Jerusalem and Palestine will turn into mere museums". Here we have to mention the great efforts made by the Latin cleric, Father Ibrahim Ayyad who published an article titled "Yitzhak Shamir falsely accuses God and History" that had a resounding reaction in Palestine and Israel.[18] Also we have to mention the Latin cleric, Monsignor Raouf Najjar, the Acting Papal Envoy in Amman who until his death in 2000 spared no effort in trying to convince the Vatican not to abandon its policy about the illegality of the Occupation and the need to end Palestinians' suffering. We have also to note the big efforts made by Afif Safieh, a son of Jerusalem and the Palestinian Ambassador in London and the Vatican through lectures, pamphlets and books related to the Arab Palestinian Cause.

During this period a strong tendency towards Arabism emerged among the ranks of Anglican Arabs which, no doubt, was a result of nationalistic tendencies that spread in the early 20th century and which was referred to by Prince Hassan in his book: *Christianity in the Arab World* when he said

> that was what Protestant missionaries did too, especially the Americans among them. They put all their efforts to have Arabic alone as the language of worship within the churches they founded or participated in founding. One of the main accomplishments of the American Evangelical Mission in Beirut was translating the Bible from the original languages to Arabic and to attract well-known Arab writers to write hymns in Arabic for church services. British Anglican missionaries, on their part, produced an Arabic text for the General Prayer Book used in their church. In Protestant schools, as in Evangelist schools also, focus was on producing all text books in Arabic. Consequently it is no coincidence that the idea of Arab Nationalism evolved at the hands of Christian Arabs, mostly Protestants or Evangelists or through a group of Christians who studied at Protestant or Evangelist schools.[19]

In the seventies, signs of this tendency showed after the church was Arabized and the reigning bishop in 1976 was Bishop Fayeq Haddad. His assistants were Bishop Aql Aql and Bishop Elia Khoury, member of the Palestinian National Council who was arrested by the Israelis and later deported to Amman. Later came Bishop Sameer Qafiti, Canon Naim Ateeq, Bishop Riyah Abu al-Asal: they were all engrossed in the Nationalist movement and the dialogue between religions.[20] Bishop Sameer Qafiti who became a member in the Royal Commission for Jerusalem's affairs in Amman, had already expanded his activities once he became the head of the Synod Council in the Middle East in 1986 through attending important international meetings and by inviting world spiritual leaders to visit Jerusalem. Among those he invited were the delegation from Britain's Churches; ex-President Jimmy Carter; Desmond Tutu, the Archbishop of South Africa; George Carey, Archbishop of Canterbury; Assembly of German churches and William Waldegrave, British Minister of State for Foreign Affairs. He also took every opportunity to raise his voice defending Palestinian rights and directing attention to the Eastern roots of Christianity and the importance of showing this at the start of the third millennium so that some people in the world stop imagining that Christianity is present only in Western-European and American culture only. [21] To stress the importance of the role of these Eastern Churches he supervised the Preparatory Conference of Asian Churches in Amman on 3 July 1996 when he declared that peace without Jerusalem would be incomplete. A complete report about the conference's agenda was published in *Al-Dustour Daily*. [22]

As for Canon Naim Ateeq, he supervised Sabeel's Centre for Theological Studies in Jerusalem; he announced the following as the principles on which the centre's work programme is based:

- Palestinian and Israeli residents of the region need and deserve peace.
- Israel must admit to the injustice it gave to Palestinians and should accept the responsibility for that.
- Palestinians should realize their democratic State with sovereignty over all the lands of the Gaza Strip and the West Bank. Israel has to withdraw to the 4 June, 1967 borders.
- Sovereignty in Jerusalem should be shared by Palestine and Israel.
- Right of return should be guaranteed for Palestinians.
- All settlements in Jerusalem, the West Bank and the Gaza Strip are illegal according to international law and should be handed over to Palestinians.

The importance of such a programme is that it shows the high intellectual and cultural level attained by the Sabeel Centre during the last few years. [23]

The third Arab bishop who took over after Bishop Qafiti's retirement in 1998 was Bishop Riyah Abu al-Asal who publicly announced the national role of Arab Christianity. He demanded the return of all confiscated endowments exactly like Israel's claims to Jewish properties in Eastern Europe. He supported the struggle of Orthodox Arabs against the sale of Orthodox endowments to Jews, stressing that Christian Arabs in Palestine are an indivisible part of the Arab nation, and that it is the duty of all to confront the despicable campaigns waged in the West against Islam and Muslims. To serve those obligations he made twenty-two tours inside the USA giving lectures and attending conventions and seminars. It addition he paid several visits to Australia, Canada and various European countries.[24]

As for the Roman Catholic Church, it is probably the second largest Christian sect in Palestine with its flock exceeding fifty thousand in number. They harboured a great resentment towards Israel because of the case of Iqret and Burum, the two villages completely destroyed by Israel immediately after the 1948 war, displacing all their residents. In 1974 Israel accused Bishop Helarion Kappucci of smuggling armaments to Palestinian commandos in his car's trunk which led to his arrest and imprisonment for a long period. He was released only after the personal intervention of Pope Paul VI. He joined the PLO and became a member of the Palestinian National Council. He started giving lectures accusing Israel of practising methods not different than those used by Nazis. His efforts were deeply appreciated all over the world especially among Arabs. He was honoured when stamps bearing his photo were issued in Sudan, Egypt, Iraq, Libya and Syria. In another direction the Arab Bishop Yousef Rayya, who succeeded Patriarch Hakeem in Palestine, was strongly criticizing Israel and urging followers of the Roman Catholic sect to sympathize with Palestinian causes. All this at the time when Bishop Lutfi Laham, who became Patriarch when Patriarch Hakeem died in 2000, was looked at by the Israeli Authorities as a member of the Popular Democratic Front for the Liberation of Palestine which was headed by Nayef Hawatmeh and opposed the Oslo Accords and resisted Israel at all levels.[25]

Bishop Helarion Kappucci is considered an important phenomenon in the Arab struggle to be liberated from Israeli occupation. He believed that the Palestinian cause is "the tragedy of an aggrieved and oppressed nation and a clergyman is disowned by his religion if he does not defend the oppressed". He described his beliefs and thoughts at a press conference he held at the Roman Catholic Diocese in Amman in early April 1994. He openly stated: "I enlisted in the service of Palestine because Jesus was the first to sacrifice himself and a student has to follow the footsteps of his mentor" and: "To live in dignity, Arabs have no choice except to liberate the Occupied Territories."

The essence of the matter is that Arab strong endeavours in resisting Israeli Occupation did not yield significant results in the face of the savage onslaught by a racist state that enjoys the full support of the US, the strongest country in the world. Arabs in Palestine were always aware of this imminent danger and called for a unified Arab Muslim-Christian stand against this sweeping current. The cause of Muslim-Christian coexistence in Jerusalem, the protection and preservation of the holy shrines and preventing them from becoming museums, as many fear, are the most serious issues facing the Arab nation that calls Arab governments to act responsibly since patience is running out. Resisting the Judaization of Jerusalem is a national obligation which is shared, these days, equally by Muslims and Christians since their existence in the whole of Palestine is in jeopardy.

In the final chapter of this book that throws some light on Jerusalem and on the Muslim-Christian presence within it for fourteen centuries I find no better words than the sombre words of 'Aref al-'Aref, Jerusalem's historian, who in 1961 said in his book *Al-Muffassal Fi Tarikh Al-Quds* (History of Jerusalem):

> you see the citizens of this land, Muslims and Christians marching towards a specific objective: thinking about the destiny of their nation and country, marching on the same track while very close together in manners, customs and also very close in their political and social principles. They have opposed the British mandate and the Jewish National Homeland not enabling colonialists to separate them. Their eternal slogan was always: (Religion is for God and Motherland is for all).

Notes:

(1) This Royal decree was published in the *Official Gazette*, Amman, 25 August, 1981

(2) As mentioned in the 1982 calendar of the Roman Orthodox Patriarchate (printed by the Roman Orthodox Patriarchate's Printing Press in Jerusalem, established in 1853)

(3) Those promises where read by Priest Costantin Qarmash, on the instructions of the Patriarch and in his presence, at the Abdali Church in Amman during the morning prayer service on 16 February, 1981. The loyal men mentioned, whom the late Patriarch Benedictus relied on, were his competitors in the election: Metropolitan Basilius and Metropolitan Jermanus

(4) *Al-Dustour Daily*, 15 January, 1992. The title of the article confirmed that the heads of nine churches called for international protection for the holy sites in Jerusalem while it published the names of seven churches only. Probably the names of the Coptic Church and the Assyrian Church were unintentionally dropped. Those two Arab churches always defended Jerusalem and their positions in Cairo and Damascus were known to all

(5) Archmenderit Atallah Hanna is a young Palestinian from the village of Romah, near Akko (Acre). Despite his accomplishment and activites he was not promoted to bishop and was not appointed to the Holy Synod. The 2001 Patriarchy Calendar mentioned him as a writer in the Arabic section

(6) The letter is signed by Yuri Mor, head of the Christian Sects Department within the Israeli Minsitry of Religion under number 989 and dated 13 May, 2000. Please note the State of Isreal's insistence on calling the Patriarchate Greek

(7) A statement made by Archmendrit Atallah Hanna to Alquds Press in Ramallah. Published in *Al-Dustour Daily* on 2 July, 2001

(8) *Al-Hayat Daily*, 1 September, 2000

(9) *Ma'ariv Daily*, 12 December, 2000

(10) as per report published in *Al-Dustour Daily*, Amman, 10 August, 1992

(11) Al-Hayat Daily, 25 December, 1998 and *Al-Rai Daily* 25 Deccember, 1998

(12) *Al-Dustour Daily*, and *Al-Arab Al-Yawm*, 17 August, 1999

(13) *Al-Dustour Daily* and *Al-Sharq Al-Awsat*, 26 December, 1999

(14) *Al-Dustour Daily*, Amman. 9 October, 2000

(15) *Al-Dustour Daily* and *Al-Rai Daily*, 20 December, 2000

(16) *Al-Rai Daily* and *Al-Arab Al-Yawm*, 26 December, 2000

(17) *Al-Dustour Daily* and *Al-Sharq Al-Awsat* 25 and 26 December, 1999 respectively

(18) *Al-Rai Daily*, Amman 10 October, 1991

(19) from an article published in *Al-Rai Daily*, Amman, 10 October, 1991

(20) Rafiq Farah, *A History of the Anglican Church in Jerusalem 1841-1991*, part 2 (Jerusalem, 1995) p.452

(21) News item about the preparatory conference of Bishopric Churches in Amman that announced that peace without Jerusalem would be incomplete. *Al-Rai Daily*, 4 July, 1996

(22) *Al-Dustour Daily*, 4 July, 1996

(23) Document published by Sabeel Centre for Theological studies early 2000

(24) Speech delivered by Bishop Riyah Abu al-Asal on the occasion of his appointment as Bishop of the Anglican Church in the Middle East on 15 August, 1998 in Jerusalem. Also his lecture at the Orthodox Club in Amman on 23 March, 1999. Published in *Al-Dustour Daily*, 31 March, 1999

(25) A detailed report in the Jerusalem Post's supplement published late September 1998

CONCLUSION

J erusalem, during the period covered by this book, was the stage for different events at the time when its Arab residents were unable to take an effective stand towards those events. The absolute Ottoman control over Bilad al-Sham was the way of life in that region which left Arabs with little room to act at a time when administrative reform that they really wished for and badly needed was starting during the Egyptian occupation of Palestine, led by Ibrahim Pasha. It was a step in the right direction yet people often found themselves in a crossfire between the dues required by the openness and development and the harsh demands of the traditionalists who through their affiliations called for loyalty towards the Muslim Caliph in Istanbul and his traditional rule.

Despite these obstacles, the period that followed the Egyptian Rule was the start of the broad openness that accompanied life in the Holy Land during the new era of friendship between the Ottoman State and the European countries who helped oust Egyptians from Bilad al-Sham. This led to the arrival of large numbers of Europeans who wanted to strengthen the presence of their churches inside the eternal city of Jerusalem. Establishing European Patriarchates and dioceses was needed to confirm presence and to gain rights and privileges, especially when it concerned holy places and shrines. That led to competition between these churches and to a steep rise in the value of land and properties benefitting the inhabitants. We must note, however, that local Christians, most of whom were Orthodox Arabs, were not greatly affected by the changes. Were it not for the spread of schools and the Russian interest in their education there would not be that national activity that sprang among them during the last decade of the 19th century and the whole of the 20th century. Arabism was more apparent among the Muslims and Christians of Jerusalem than in other places. It was the phenomenon backed by all, without exception, as per the slogan "Religion is for God and Motherland is for all".

Since the Omari Covenant, Jerusalem has always been an Arab, Palestinian Muslim-Christian city that has a special place in the hearts of each Arab due to its holiness and religious status. Christian presence in it, since the emergence of Islam, always accompanied Muslim presence. The city became a symbol of diversity, centrism and peaceful coexistence among followers of different religions. The Zionist invasion of Palestine in the 20th century provided a dark page in history due to the sufferings it created in the Holy Land by its aggression and its expansionist policies and greed resisted by all Arabs, Muslim and Christians who are seeking justice and preservation of their rights and legacies. Hundreds of thousands have signed the Covenant of Jerusalem adopted by Jerusalemites on 31 July, 2000. It was preceded by a statement issued by the Muslim-Christian meeting that took place in the Orient House in Jerusalem on 29 July, 2000 as a token of the eternal ties between Muslims and Christians under the canopy of Jerusalem which will be always protected by God.

APPENDIX

The Greek Orthodox Patriarchate
Jerusalem

A list of the properties of the Greek Orthodox Patriarchate of Jerusalem in the occupied West Bank and Gaza Strip:

Churches and Monasteries

Churches:
1. Church of the Holy Sepulchre in Jerusalem
2. Church of Nativity – Bethlehem
3. Church of St George – Bethlehem
4. Church of Gethsemane – Jerusalem
5. Church of Lazarus – Gethsemane
6. Mar Elias Church – Jerusalem – Bethlehem Road
7. Church of Saints Constantine and Helen within the Central Monastery
8. Saint Theodosius' Church within Ben Ubaid Monastery
9. Saint Elijah's Church in Jericho
10. Mar Mitri's Church
11. Church of St Onophrius
12. Church of St Stephanos
13. Church of the Holy Trinity in Toubas (Jinin District)
14. Church of Mother of God Dormition in Zababdeh
15. St George's Church at Wadi Al-Qilt – Jericho
16. Shepherds' Church – Beit Sahour

17. Forefathers' Church – Beit Sahour
18. Church of Bayt Naji's Monastery – Jerusalem
19. Church of Galilee's Monastery – Mount of Olives

Patriarch's Headquarters
20. Church of Saint Jacob – Jerusalem
21. Church of St Taqla within the Central Monastery in Jerusalem
22. Church of Saint Modestos in Abu Thor
23. Church of St Khareton in Ain Farah
24. Church of Dayr Sidnaya in Jerusalem
25. Church of the Monastery of Christ's Jail
26. St Catherine's Church
27. St Michael's Church
28. St Spirodon's Church
29. St Basilius' Church
30. St George's Church in Al-Khader Village
31. St Porpherius' Church in Gaza
32. Church of Christ's Transfiguration in Ramallah
33. St George's Church in Beit Jala
34. Church of the Mother of God in Beit Jala
35. Church of the Archangels in Beit Jala
36. St Nicholas' Church in Beit Jala
37. St George's Church in Jifna
38. St George's Church in Taibeh
39. St Dimitri's Church in Nablus
40. Church of Incense Carriers
41. St George's Church in Rafidia
42. St George's Church in Tulkarem
43. Church of the Dormition of the Mother of God in Ain Ureik
44. Church of the Mother of God in Aboud
45. Church of our Lady the Virgin opposite the Holy Sepulchre

Monasteries and Convents
1. The Central Monastery of the Greek Orthodox Patriarchate in Jerusalem
2. Monastery of our Father Abraham in Jerusalem
3. St Spirodon's Monastery in Jerusalem
4. St Nicholas' Monastery in Jerusalem

5. Monastery of Sidnaya in Jerusalem
6. St Mikhail's Monastery
7. Monastery of Galilee / Patriarchate Headquarters at Tur Mountain
8. Mar Saba Monastery
9. Monastery of Ben Obaid
10. Glakton Monastery
11. St George's Monastery
12. St Grasimo's Monastery
13. Bayt Naji Monastery
14. Jericho Monastery
15. Gaza Monastery
16. Al-Khader Monastery
17. Beit Jala Monastery
18. Alaizariyyah Monastery
19. Prophet Elias' Monastery – Jerusalem – Bethlehem Road
20. Ramallah's Ministry
21. Monastery at the Mount of Temptations – Jericho
22. Bethlehem's Monastery
23. St Kharalombos' Monastery
24. Monastery of St John the Baptist
25. St Theodorus' Monastery
26. St George's Monastery – known as the Hospital
27. St Catherine's Monastery
28. St Nicodimus' Monastery
29. Monastery of the Incarceration of Christ
30. St Inofrius' Monastery
31. Monastery of Zion
32. St Stephanos' Monastery
33. Convent of the Lady – known as Girls Convent
34. Monastery of Sidnaya
35. St Ephthemius' Monastery
36. Jacob's Well Monastery – Nablus
37. The Greek Orthodox Monastery – Tulkarem

Agreement between the Holy See and the State of Israel Pursuant to Article 3 § (3) of the Fundamental Agreement between the Holy See and the State of Israel (also referred to as the "Legal Personality Agreement")

Article 1

This Agreement is made on the basis of the provisions of the "Fundamental Agreement between the State of Israel and the Holy See", which was signed on 30 December 1993, and then entered into force on 10 March 1994 (hereinafter: the "Fundamental Agreement").

Article 2

Recalling that the Holy See is the Sovereign Authority of the Catholic Church, the State of Israel agrees to assure full effect in Israeli law to the legal personality of the Catholic Church itself.

Article 3

§1. The State of Israel agrees to assure full effect in Israeli law, in accordance with the provisions of this Agreement, to the legal personality of the following:

(a) these Eastern Catholic Patriarchates: the Greek Melkite Catholic, the Syrian Catholic, the Maronite, the Chaldean, the Armenian Catholic (hereinafter: the "Eastern Catholic Patriarchates");

(b) the Latin Patriarchate of Jerusalem, id est the Latin Patriarchal Diocese of Jerusalem;

(c) the present Dioceses of the Eastern Catholic Patriarchates;

(d) new Dioceses, wholly in Israel, Eastern Catholic or Latin, as may exist from time to time;

(e) the "Assembly of the Catholic Ordinaries of the Holy Land".

§2. The Holy See states, for the avoidance of doubt, that the listing in par. 1 does not prejudice in any way the established order of precedence of the Heads of the various entities, according to their personal rank and as it is fixed by traditional usage and accepted by them.

§3. For the avoidance of doubt, it is stated that the question of assuring full effect in Israeli law to the legal personality of any new cross-border Diocese is left open.

§4. For the purposes of this Agreement, a Parish is in integral part of the respective Diocese, and, without affecting its status under the canon law, will not acquire a separate legal personality under Israeli law. A Diocese may, subject to the canon law, authorise its Parishes to act on its behalf, in such matters and under such terms, as it may determine.

§5. In this Agreement, "Diocese" includes its synonyms or equivalents.

Article 4

The State of Israel agrees to assure full effect in Israeli law, in accordance with the provisions of this Agreement, to the legal personality of the Custody of the Holy Land.

Article 5

The State of Israel agrees to assure full effect in Israeli law, in accordance with the provisions of this Agreement, to the legal personality of the following, as they exist from time to time in Israel:

(a) the Pontifical Institutes of Consecrated Life of the kinds that exist in the Catholic Church, and such of their Provinces or Houses as the Institute concerned may cause to be certified;

(b) other official entities of the Catholic Church.

Article 6

§1. For the purposes of this Agreement the legal persons referred to in Articles 3-5 (hereinafter, in this Article: "legal person"), being established under the canon law, are deemed to have been created according to the legislation of the Holy See, being Sovereign in international law.

§2. (a) the law which governs any legal transaction or other legal acts in Israel between any legal person and any party shall be the law of the State of Israel, subject to the provisions of sub-paragraph (b).

(b) any matter concerning the identity of the head, of the presiding officer or of any other official or functionary of a legal person, or their authority or their powers to act on behalf of the legal person, is governed by the canon law.

(c) without derogation from the generality of sub-paragraph (b), certain kinds of transactions by a legal person concerning immovable property or certain other kinds of property, depend on a prior written permission of the Holy See in accordance with Its written Decisions as issued from time to time. Public access to the aforesaid Decisions will be in accordance with the Implementation Provisions.

§3. (a) any dispute concerning an internal ecclesiastical matter between a member, official or functionary of a legal person and any legal person, whether the member, official or functionary belongs to it or not, or between legal persons, shall be determined in accordance with the canon law, in a judicial or administrative ecclesiastical forum.

(b) For the avoidance of doubt it is stated that the provisions of 2(a) shall not apply to disputes referred to in the above sub paragraph (a).

§4. for the avoidance of doubt, it is stated:

(a) a legal person, whose legal personality is given full effect in Israel, is deemed to have consented to sue and be sued before a judicial or administrative forum in Israel, if that is the proper forum under Israeli law.

(b) sub-paragraph (a) does not derogate from any provision in Articles 6-9.

Article 7

The application of this Agreement to any legal person is without prejudice to any of its rights or obligations previously created.

Article 8

§1. For the avoidance of doubt, nothing in this Agreement shall be construed as supporting an argument that any of the legal persons to which this Agreement applies had not been a legal person prior to this Agreement.

§2. If a party makes a claim that such a legal person had not been a legal person in Israeli law prior to this Agreement, that party shall bear the burden of proof.

Article 9

Should a question with regard to the canon law arise in any matter before a Court or forum other than in a forum of the Catholic Church, it shall be regarded as a question of fact.

Article 10

The terms "ecclesiastical" and "canon law" refer to the Catholic Church and Its law.

Article 11

§1. Without derogating from any provision, declaration or statement in the Fundamental Agreement, the ecclesiastical legal persons in existence at the time of the entry of this Agreement into force are deemed as being legal persons in accordance with the provisions of this Agreement, if listed in the ANNEXES to this Agreement, which are specified in par. 4.

§2. The ANNEXES form, for all intents and purposes, an integral part of this Agreement.

§3. The ANNEXES will include the official name, respective date or year of establishment in the Catholic Church, a local address and, if the head office is abroad, also its address.

§4. (a) ANNEX I lists the legal persons to which Article 3(1)(a, b, c, e) and Article 4 apply, as the case may be;

(b) ANNEX II lists the legal persons to which Article 5(a) applies;

(c) ANNEX III lists the legal persons to which Article 5(b) applies.

Article 12

The other matters on which the Parties have agreed are included in the Schedule to this Agreement, named "Implementation Provisions", which forms, for all intents and purposes, an integral part of this Agreement, and references to the Agreement include the Schedule.

Article 13

This Agreement shall enter into force on the date of the latter notification of ratification by a Party.

Done in two original copies in the English and Hebrew languages, both texts being equally authentic. In case of divergence, the English text shall prevail, except where explicitly provided otherwise in the Schedule.

Signed in _____ , this _____ day of the month of _____ in the year _____, which corresponds to the _____ day of the month of _____ in the year _____

The Annexes
(Article 11)

Ref: Article 3 § 1 (a)

Greek Melkite Catholic Patriarchate of Antioch
Head: His Beatitude Patriarch Maximos V HAKIM
    Bab Touma P.O.B. 22249 - Damascus - Syria
Local address: P.O.B. 14130 - Greek Catholic Patriarchate Street 91141
    Jerusalem

Syrian Catholic Patriarchate of Antioch
Head: His Beatitude Patriarch Ignace Antoine II HAYEK
    Rue de Damas P.O.B. 116-5087 - Beyrouth - Lebanon
Local address: P.O.B. 19787 - Chaldeans Street, 6 - 91191 Jerusalem

Maronite Patriarchate of Antioch
Head: His Eminence and Beatitude Patriarch Nlasrallah Pierre Cardinal SFEIR
    Bkerké - Lebanon
Local address: P.O.B.14219 - Maronite Convent Street, 25 Jerusalem

Chaldean Patriarchate of Babylon
Head: His Beatitude Patriarch Raphael BIDAWID
    Al Mansour P.O.B. 6112 - Baghdad - Iraq
Local address: P.O.B. 20108 - Chaldeans Street, 5 - 91200 Jerusalem

Armenian Catholic Patriarchate of Cilicia
Head: His Beatitude Patriarch Jean Pierre XVIII KASPARIAN
    rue de l'Hôpital Libanais, Jeitaoui 2400 Beyrouth - Lebanon
Local address: P.O.B. 19546 - Via Dolorosa, 41 Jerusalem

Ref: Article 3 § 1 (b)

Latin Patriarchate of Jerusalem
id est Latin Patriarchal Diocese of Jerusalem
established by the Holy See in 1847
Head: His Beatitude Patriarch Michel SABBAH
    P.O.B. 14152 - Latin Patriarchate Street 91141 Jerusalem

Ref: Article 3 § 1 (c)

Greek Melkite Catholic Patriarchal Exarchate of Jerusalem
established in 1834, by the Greek Melkite Catholic Patriarch of Antioch
Head: His Excellency Archbishop Lutfi LAHAM
    P.O.B. 14130 - Greek Catholic Patriarchate Street 91141 Jerusalem

Greek Melkite Catholic Archeparchy of Akka, St. John of Acre, Ptolemais
established in 1752, by the Greek Melkite Catholic Patriarch of Antioch
Head: His Excellency Archbishop Maximos SALLOUM
    P.O.B. 279 - 32 Hagefen Street 31002 Haifa

Greek Melkite Catholic Archeparchy of Baniyas, Caesarea Philippi, Paneas
established in 1964, by the Greek Melkite Catholic Patriarch of Antioch
Head: His Excellency Archbishop Antoine HAYEK
    Archevêché de Paneas, Jdeidet Marjeyoun, Lebanon
Local address: The Greek Melkite Catholic Parish, Metulla

Syrian Catholic Patriarchal Exarchate of Jerusalem
established in 1845, by the Syrian Catholic Patriarch of Antioch
Head: His Excellency Bishop Pierre ABDEL-AHAD
    P.O.B. 19787 - Chaldeans Street 6 91191 Jerusalem

Maronite Archeparchy of Haifa and the Holy Land
established in 1996, by the Maronite Patriarch of Antioch
Head: His Excellency Archbishop Paul Nabil SAYYAH
Local address: P.O.B. 1442 - Roubin Street 5 - 31000 Haifa

Maronite Patriarchal Exarchate of Jerusalem
established in 1895, by the Maronite Patriarch of Antioch
Head: His Excellency Archbishop Paul Nabil SAYYAH
P.O.B. 14219 - Maronite Convent Street, 25 Jerusalem

Armenian Catholic Patriarchal Exarchate of Jerusalem
established in 1856, by the Armenian Catholic Patriarch of Cilicia
Head: His Excellency Bishop André BEDOGLOUYAN
P.O.B. 19546 - Via Dolorosa, 41 Jerusalem

Ref: Article 3 § 1 (c)

The Assembly of the Catholic Ordinaries of the Holy Land
established in 1992, by the Holy See
Presiding Officer: The Latin Patriarch of Jerusalem pro tempore
c/o Notre Dame of Jerusalem Center
P.O.B. 20531 - 91204 Jerusalem

Ref: Article 4

The Custody of the Holy Land (Custodia Terrae Sanctae)
established in 1342, by the Holy See
Presiding Officer: The Custos of the Holy Land Most Rev. Father Giuseppe
NAZZARO, OFM
P.O.B. 186 - Saint Francis Street, 1 - 91001 Jerusalem

ANNEX II
(ARTICLE 11 § 4.B)

Ref: Article 5 (a)

Augustinians of the Assumption (Assumptionists)
established in 1864
Local address: Shrine of Saint Peter in Gallicantu, Ma'aleh Hashalom - Mount
Zion - P.O.B. 31653 - 91316 Jerusalem
Head Office: Via San Pio V, 55 - 00165 Rome, Italy
Basilian Order of the Most Holy Saviour (of the Melkites) (Salvatorians)
established in 1717
Local address: Aïn Dor Street 23 - P.O.B.9133 - 31091 Haifa
Head Office: Couvent Mar Elias - Jiita - Lebanon

Basilian Sisters "Chouérites"
established in 1734
Local address: Nabaa Street - P.O.B. 99 - 16000 Nazareth
Head Office: Couvent Notre-Dame de l'Annonciation Zouk-Michael - Lebanon

Benedictine Abbey of the dormition
established in 1906
P.O.B. 22, Mount Zion - Jerusalem

Benedictine Congregation of Saint Mary of Mount Olivet
established in 1344
Local address: Resurrection Church - Abu Gosh - P.O.B. 407 - 91003 Jerusalem
Head Office: Abbazia di Monte Oiiveto Maggiore 53020 Chiusure - Italy

Benedictine Sisters of the Eucharistic King
established in 1986
Local address: Benedictine Priory of Tabgha - P.O.B. 52 - 14100 Tiberias
Head Office: 30 Banahaw St. - Cubao - 1109 Quezon City - Philippines

Bethany Sisters of the Imitation of Christ
established in 1950
Local address: Saint Thomas Church - P.O.B. 19787 - 91191 Jerusalem

Head Office: Bethany Convent, Kalathipady - Vadavathoor
686010 Kerala - India

Carmelite Sisters of "Sainte Thérèse de Florence"
established in 1874
Local address: Italian Street 10 - P.O.B. 9037 - 33266 Haifa
Head Office: Via Bernardo Rucellai, 1 - 50123 Firenze - Italy

Carmelite Sisters of Saint Joseph
established in 1872
Local address: Carmel Saint Joseph - P.O.B. 8 - 30090 Isfia - Mount Carmel
Head Office: 71118 Saint Martin Belle Roche - France

Christian Brothers de La Salle
established in 1725
Local address: Collège des Frères - Yefet Street 23 - P.O.B. 8251 - 61082 Jaffa
Head Office: Via Aurelia 476 - C.P. 9099 - 00100 Rome - Italy

Cistercian Order of the Strict Observance (Trappists)
Trappist Abbey "Notre Dame des Douleurs"
established in 1890
Local address: Abbaye de Latroun - Poste mobile - Shimshon 99762
Head Office: Viale Africa, 33 - 00144 Rome - Italy

Company of the Daughters of Charity of St. Vincent de Paul
established in 1633
Local address: Allenby Street 13 - P.O.B. 2106 - 33092 Haifa
Head Office: 140, rue du Bac - 75340 Paris - France

Congregation of the Mission (Lazarist Fathers)
established in 1632
Local address: Lazarist Fathers Convent - 20 Agron Street
P.O.B. 1144 - 91010 Jerusalem
Head Office: Via dei Capasso, 30 - 00164 Rome - Italy

Congregation of the Passion of Jesus Christ (Passionist Fathers)
established in 1741

Local address: Ash-Shayyah St. - Bethany - P.O.B. 19087 - 91190 Jerusalem
Head Office: Piazza SS. Giovanni e Paolo 13 - 00184 Rome - Italy

Daughters of Mary Auxiliatrix (Salesian Sisters)
established in 1872
Local address: P.O.B. 73 - Nazareth
Head Office: Via dell'Ateneo Salesiano 81 - 00139 Rome - Italy

Daughters of Our Lady of Mount Calvary
established in 1827
Local address: Mount of Olives - P.O.B. 19199 - 91191 Jerusalem
Head Office: Via Emanuele Filiberto, 104 - 00185 Rome - Italy

Daughters of Our Lady of Sorrows
established in 1930
Local address: Abu Diss - P.O.B. 19257 - 91192 Jerusalem
Head Office: Maison Marie Saint Frai - 65000 Tarbes - France

Daughters of Saint Anne
established in 1866
Local address: Meir Street 11 - P.O.B. 9127 - 35056 Haifa
Head Office: Via Merulana 177 - 00185 Rome - Italy

Discalced Carmelite Sisters - Monastery "Notre Dame du Mont Carmel"
established in 1892
Tchernikhowski Road, 2 - P.O.B. 9047 - 31090 Haifa

Discalced Carmelite Sisters - Monastery "Pater Noster"
established in 1873
Mount of Olives - P.O.B. 19064 - 91190 Jerusalem

Discalced Carmelite Sisters - Monastery "Sainte Famille"
established in 1910
Street 125/4 - P.O.B. 22 - 16100 Nazareth

Dominican Sisters of Charity of Tours, of the Presentation of the Blessed Virgin
established in 1696

Local address: Maison d'Abraham - Ras el-Amoud
              P.O.B. 19680 - 91196 Jerusalem
Head Office: Via Valdieri, 4 - 00135 Rome - Italy

Franciscan Missionary Sisters of Mary (White Sisters)
established in 1877
Local address: Givat Yam 4/34 - Herzl Street - 59301 Beit-Yam
Head Office: Via Giusti, 12 - 00185 Rome - Italy

Franciscan Missionary Sisters of the Immaculate Heart of Mary (Sisters of Egypt)
established in 1868
Local address: P.O.B. 302 - Nazareth
Head Office: Via Caterina Troiani 90 - 00144 Rome - Italy

Franciscan Sisters of the Eucharist
established in 1973
Local address: Mount of Olives Road, 42 - P.O.B. 230 - Jerusalem
Head Office: 405 Allen Avenue - Meridan - Connecticut 06450 - USA

Franciscan Sisters of the Heart of Jesus
established in 1946,
Local address: Saint Saviour Convent - New Gate - P.O.B. 186 - Jerusalem
Head Office: House of Charity - Palm Street - Victoria - Gozo - Malta

Franciscan Sisters of the Holy Cross of Lebanon
established in 1967
Local address: St. Francis Street, 13 - P.O.B. 14558 - 91145 Jerusalem
Head Office: Couvent de la Croix - Jall-Eddib - (Meten) - Lebanon

Fraternity of the Little Sisters of Jesus
established in 1949
Province of the Holy land
Local address: Paul VI Street, 42 - P.O.B. 1531 - Nazareth
Province of Israel
Local address: Bethlehem Road 17 - P.O.B. 10203 - 16115 Jerusalem
Head Office: Tre Fontane - Via di Acque Salvie, 2 - 00142 Rome - Italy

Hospitaller Order of St. John of God (Fatebenefratelli)
established in 1571
Local address: Holy Family Hospital - Road 727/1 - P.O.B. 8 - 16100 Nazareth
Head Office: Via della Nocetta, 263 - 00164 Rome - Italy

Institute of the Blessed Virgin Mary (Mary Ward Sisters)
established in 1703
Local address: Nablus Road 2 - P.O.B. 19070 - 91190 Jerusalem
Head Office: Via Nomentana 250 - 00162 Rome - Italy

Lebanese Maronlte Order (Baladites)
established in 1695
Local address: Couvent Saint Antoine - Hadolfin Street, 22
P.O.B. 41077 - 68034 Jaffa
Head Office: Couvent Saint Antoine - Gazir - Lebanon

Little Brothers of Jesus
established in 1957
Local address: Givat Hamore - P.O.B. 523 - 18105 Afula
Head Office: 97 Sudbourne Road - London SW2 5AF - England

Maronite Antonine Order
established in 1742
Local address: Ash-Shayyah Street - Bethany - P.O.B. 803 - Jerusalem
Head Office: Saint Roch - Dekwaneh - Beirut - Lebanon

Maronite Antonine Sisters
established in 1940
Local address: Ramallah Street, Beit Hanina, Jerusalem
Head Office: Couvent Mar Doumith - B.P. 84 - Roumié - Lebanon

Missionaries of Africa (White Fathers)
established in 1878
Local address: Shrine of Saint Anne - P.O.B. 19079 - 91190 Jerusalem
Head Office: Via Aurelia, 269 - C.P. 9078 - 00165 Rome - Italy

Missionary Daughters of Calvary
established in 1924
Local address: Colegio Español de Nuestra Señora del Pilar
P.O.B. 14250 - 91142 Jerusalem
Head Office: Via Marino Campagna 129 - 00140 Rocca di Papa - Italy

Missionary Sisters of the Catechism
established in 1939
Local address: Casa Nova Street - P.O.B. 1321 - 91013 Jerusalem
Head Office: Via Mattia de Rossi 2 - 00040 Ariccia - Italy

Missionary Sisters "Pie Madri della Nigrizia" (Suore Comboniane)
established in 1897
Local address: Bethany - P.O.B. 19504 - Jerusalem
Head Office: Via di Boccea 506 - P.O.B. 9067 - 00166 Rome - Italy

Oblate Nuns of the Congregation of Saint Mary of Mount Olivet
established in 1977
Monastère Ste Françoise Romaine - Abu Gosh - P.O.B. 407- 91003 Jerusalem

Order of Friars Minor Capuchin
established in 1528
Local address: The Franciscan Capuchin Friary
18 Disraeli Street - Talbiye - 92222 Jerusalem
Head Office: Via Piemonte 70 - 00187 Rome - Italy

Order of Preachers (Dominicans)
established in 1216
Local address: Shivtei Israel Road, 8 - P.O.B. 298 - 97605 Jerusalem
Head Office: Piazza Pietro d'Illiria, 1 - 00153 Rome - Italy

Order of the Discalced Brothers of the Blessed Virgin Mary of Mt. Carmel (Carmelites)
established in 1593
Local address: "Stella Maris" Monastery P.O.B. 9047 - 31090 Haifa
Head Office: Corso d'Italia, 38 - 00198 Rome - Italy

Poor Clares - Monastery "Sainte Claire"
established in 1888
Chanoch Albeck Street, 1 P.O.B. 1013 - 91009 Jerusalem

Poor Clares - Monastery "Sainte Claire"
established in 1884
Poste restante - 16000 Nazareth

Religieuses de L'Assomption (Religious of the Assumption)
established in 1867
Local address: Saint Peter in Gallicantu Ma'aleh Hashalom
                    P.O.B. 31653 - 91316 Jerusalem
Head Office: 17, rue de l'Assomption - 75016 Paris - France

Religious of Nazareth
established in 1853
Local address: Near the Basilica, 4/306 P. O. B. 274 - Nazareth
Head Office: Via CaterinaFieschi, 6 - 00151 Rome- Italy

Religious of Our Lady of Zion
established in 1856
Local address: "Ecce Homo" Convent - Via Dolorosa, 41
                    P.O.B. 19056 - 91190 Jerusalem
Head Office: Via Garibaldi, 28 - 00153 Rome - Italy

Sacred Heart Fathers of Betharram
established in 1877
Local address: P.O.B. 22 - 16100 Nazareth
Head Office: Via A. Brunetti 27 - 00186 Rome - Italy

Salesians of Don Bosco
established in 1874
Local address: Beit Jamal P. O. B. 12 - 99101 Bet Shemesh
Head Office: Via della Pisana 1111 - 00163 Rome - Italy

Salvatorian Sisters of Our Lady of the Annunciation (of the Melkites)
established in 1940

Local address: House of Providence - Allenby Road 36 - Haifa
Head Office: Couvent Saint Sauveur - Saida - Lebanon

Sisters of Charity of Jesus and Mary
established in 1803
Local address: Street No. 24, 30 - P.O.B. 10 - 30090 Isfya
Head Office: 25 rue Saint Bernard - 1060 Bruxelles - Belgium

Sisters of Charity of Saint Charles Borromeo
established in 1652
Local address: St Charles Hospice - Lloyd George Street 12
Head Office: Kloster Grafschaft - 57392 Schmallenberg - Germany

Sisters of Charity of Saints Bartolomea Capitanio and Vincenza Gerosa (Sisters of "Maria Bambina")
established in 1840
Local address: Holy Family Hospital - Road 727/1 - P.O.B. 8 - 16100 Nazareth
Head Office: Via S. Sofia, 13 - 20122 Milano - Italy

Sisters of Charity of the Immaculate Conception (Suore d'Ivrea)
established in 1904
Local Address: Annunciation Convent - P.O.B. 214-16101 Nazareth
Head Office: Via della Renella, 85 - 00153 Rome - Italy

Sisters of Our Divine Saviour (Salvatorian Sisters, Salvator Mundi)
established in 1888
Local address: P.O.B. 121 - 16101 Nazareth
Head Office: Viale Mura Gianicolensi 67 - 00152 Rome - Italy

Sisters of Our Lady of Mercy ("Mercedarie")
established in 1864
Local address: Mount Tabor - Dahbourye - P.O.B. 16 - Nazareth
Head Office: 24 Via Ostriana - 00199 Rome - Italy

Sisters of Saint Elizabeth
established in 1887
Local address: Dom Polski, Hahoma Hashlishit Street 8

P.O.B. 277 - 91200 Jerusalem
Head Office: Via Nomentana Rome - Italy

Sisters of Saint Joseph of the Apparition
established in 1848
Province of Israel
Local address: Our Lady, Ark of the Covenant, Rehov Notre-Dame - Kiryat-
Yearim - P.O.B. 32233 - 91003 Jerusalem
Province of the Holy Land
Local address: Saint Joseph Hospital - P.O.B. 19264 - 91192 Jerusalem
Head Office: 90 Avenue Foch - 94120 Fontenay sous Bois - France

Sisters of the Holy Cross
established in 1841
Local address: "Mater Ecclesiae" Center - Dona Gracia Street
P.O.B. 207 - 14101 Tiberias
Head Office: St Mary's Notre Dame - Indiana 46556 - USA

Sisters of the Holy Cross "de Chavanod"
established in 1932
Local address: Betharram House - P.O.B. 22 - 16100 Nazareth
Head Office: 8, rue Alcide Zentzer - CH-1211 Geneva 4 - Switzerland

Sisters of the Holy Family of Nazareth
established in 1875
Local address: Latin Vicariate - 16100 Nazareth
Head Office: Via Nazareth 400 - 00166 Rome - Italy

Society of Jesus (Jesuits)
established in 1540
Local address: Emile Botta Street, 3 - P.O.B. 497 - 91004 Jerusalem
Head Office: Borgo S. Spirito 4 - 00193 Rome - Italy

Teaching Sisters of Saint Dorothy (Daughters of the Sacred Hearts)
established in 1905
Local address: Deir Rafat - P.O.B. 275 - 99100 Beit Shemesh
Head Office: Via S. Domenico 23 - 36100 Vicenza - Italy

The Congregation of the Rosary Sisters of Jerusalem
established in 1885
Agron Street, 14 - P.O.B. 54 - 94190 Jerusalem

The Servants of Charity Congregation (Opera Don Guanella)
established in 1928
Local address: Opera Don Guanella - Paul VI Road
      P.O.B. 1586 - 16115 Nazareth
Head Office: Vicolo Clementi - 00148 Rome - Italy

ANNEX III
(Article 11 § 4.c)

Ref: Article 5(b)

(a) Institutes of Consecrated Life and Ecclesial Movements:

Community of the Beatitudes
established in 1976 under the Archbishop of Alby, France
Local address: 15 Hamefaked Street - P.O.B. 32285 - 91322 Jerusalem
Head Office: Couvent Notre-Dame - 81170 Cordes - France

Community of "The Work" (Das Werk)
established in 1975 under the Bishop of Feldkirch, Austria
Local address: Shrine of Saint Anne - P.O.B. 19079 - 91190 Jerusalem
Head Office: Thalbachgasse 10 - A.6900 Bregenz - Austria

Consolers of Gethsemani
established in 1931 under the Archbishop of Vienna, Austria
Local address: Apostolic Delegation - Mount of Olives
P.O.B. 19199 - 91191 Jerusalem
Head Office: Rennweg 63 - Vienna - Austria

"Institutión Teresiana"
established in 1924 under the Holy See
Local address: Baha El Din Street - P.O.B. 19256 - 91192 Jerusalem
Head Office: Via Monte Pramaggiore 8 - Rome - Italy
Little Family of the Annunciation
established in 1972 under the Archbishop of Bologna, Italy
Local address: Ras El Amoud - P.O.B. 20776 - 91200 Jerusalem
Head Office: Via Casaglia, 7 - 40043 Marzabotto - Italy

Little Family of the Resurrection
established in 1986 under the Bishop of Cesena-Sarsina, Italy
Local address: Mount of Olives P.O.B. 51398 - Jerusalem
Head Office: Valleripa 5, - 47020 Linaro - Italy

Maronlte Sisters of "Sainte Thérèse de l'Enfant Jesus"
established in 1935 under the Maronite Patriarch of Antioch
Local address: Foyer Mar Maroun - Maronite Convent Street 25
P.O.B. 14219 - 91141 Jerusalem
Head Office: Kleat - Kesrouan - Lebanon

Missionary Sisters of Our Lady of Fatima
established in 1964 under the Archbishop of Rio de Janeiro, Brazil
Local address: Terra Sancta Convent - Bialik Street - P.O.B. 19 - 72100 Ramleh
Head Office: Rua Mentor Conto 554 - Barro Verunello
San Gusallo - 24415 Rio de Janeiro - Brazil

Monks of the Theophany
established in 1980 under the Greek Melkite Catholic Patriarch of Antioch
Monastery "Saint Jean du Désert" - P.O.B. 9048 - 91090 Jerusalem

Nuns of Bethlehem and of the Assumption of the Virgin
established in 1951 under the Bishop of Gubbio, Italy
Local address: Monastère Notre-Dame de l'Assomption - Beit Jemal
P.O.B. 525 - 99101 Beit Shemesh
Head Office: Monastère Notre-Dame du Buisson Ardent, Currière en Chartreuse
38380 St. Laurent du Pont - France

Nuns of the Annunciation
established in 1958 under the Greek Melkite Catholic Eparch of Akko
Street 5093, No. 3 - P.O.B. 216 - 16101 Nazareth

Religious of "Lavra Netofa"
established in 1963 under the Greek Melkite Catholic Eparch of Akko
Melkite Monastery of Lower Galilee - P.O.B. 211 - 24973 Deir Hanna

Religious of Our Lady of Sion
established in 1855 under the Archbishop of São Paulo, Brazil
Local address: Shmuel Hanaggid Street 26 P.O.B. 768 - Jerusalem
Head Office: Rua Costa Aguiar 1264 04204001 São Paulo - Brazil

Sisters of Holy Cross of Jerusalem
established in 1963 under the Bishop of Beauvais, France
Local address: St. John in Montana - Ein Karem P.O.B. 1704 – 95744 Jerusalem
Head Office: Le Prieuré - 60820 Boran sur Oise - France

The Silent Workers of the Cross
established in 1960 under the Bishop of Ariano-Irpino, Italy
Local address: "Mater Misericordiae" House - Ash-Shayyah Street
P.O.B. 19638 - Jerusalem
Head Office: Via dei Bresciani, 2 - 00186 Rome - Italy

Work of Mary - Focolare/ Opera di Maria - Focolare
established in 1964 under the Holy See
* Women's branch
Local address: Iskandar Khoury Street 5 P.O.B. 472 - 91003 Jerusalem
* Men's branch
Local address: Nablus Road 5 P. O. B . 1794 - 91017 Jerusalem
Head Office: Via di Frascati 302 - 00040 Rocca di Papa - Italy

(b) Institutes of Higher Education:

Ecumenical Institute for Theological Studies ("TANTUR")
established in 1966 under the Holy See
Local address: Hebron Road - Ha RosmcrinP.O.B. 19556 - 91194 Jerusalem
Head Office: University of Notre Dame, Notre Dame - Indiana 46556 - USA

Institut Saint Pierre de Sion - Ratisbonne
established in 1873 under the Holy See
Shmuel Hanagid Street, 26 - P.O.B. 7336 - 91072 Jerusalem

Pontifical Biblical Institute
established in 1927 under the Holy See
Local address: Emile Botta Street, 3 - P.O.B. 497 - 91004 Jerusalem
Head Office: Pontificio Istituto Biblico, Via della Pilotta, 25 - 00187 Rome - Italy

Pontifical University of Salamanca
established in 1940 under the Holy See
Local address: Institut Biblique et Archéologique Espagnol, Sheyah Street
P.O.B. 19030 - 91130 Jerusalem
Head Office: Compania 5 - 37008 Salamanca - Spain

Pontificium Athenaeum "Antonianum"
established in 1901 under the Holy See
Local address: Studium Biblicum Franciscanum, Via Dolorosa
P.O.B. 19424 - 91193 Jerusalem
Head Office: Via Merulana 124-00185 Rome - Italy

Pontificium Athenaeum "Sant'Anselmo"
established in 1914 under the Holy See
Local address: "Theologisches Studienjahr Jerusalem Dormition Abbey"
Mount Zion - P.O.B. 22 - Jerusalem
Head Office: Piazza dei Cavalieri di Malta, 5 - 00153 Rome - Italy

Salesian Pontifical University
established in 1940 under the Holy See
Local address: Salesian Center of Theological Studies Cremisan
P.O.B. 10457 - 91104 Jerusalem
Head Office: Piazza dell' Ateneo Salesiano, 1 - 00139 Rome - Italy

The French Biblical and Archaeological School of Jerusalem
"Ecole Biblique et Archeologique Française de Jerusalem"
established in 1892 under the Holy See
Nablus Road, 6 - P.O.B. 19053 - 91190 Jerusalem

(c) Other Official Entities:

Archdiocese of Cologne
established in VIII century under the Holy See
Local address: Shrine of Tabgha "Mensa Christi" P.O.B. 52 - 14100 Ti-berias
Head Office: Marzellenstrasse 32 - Cologne I - Germany

Archdiocese of Warsaw
established in 1798 under the Holy See
Local address: Dom Polski - 8 Hahoma Hashlishit Street
P.O.B. 277 - 91200 Jerusalem
Head Office: ul. Miodowa 17,00-246 Warsaw - Poland

"Associazione Nazionale per Soccorere i Missionari Italiani" (A.N.S.M.I.)
established in 1886 under the Holy See
Local address: Lohamey Hagettaot Street 12 - 31091 Haifa
Head Office: Via Cavour, 256 - 00184 Rome - Italy

Austrian Hospice of the Holy Family
established in 1853 under the Archbishop of Vienna
Local address: Via Dolorosa P.O.B. 19600 - 91194 Jerusalem
Head Office: Wollzeile 2, A-1010 Vienna - Austria

Caritas Jerusalem
established in 1967 under the Latin Patriarch of Jerusalem
Shivtei Israel Road, 8 - P.O.B. 20894 - 97200 Jerusalem

"Casa de Santiago"
established in 1996 under the Spanish Bishops' Conference
Local address: Sheyah Street - P.O.B. 19030 - 91190 Jerusalem
Head Office: Añastro, 1 - P.O.B. 29075 - 28033 Madrid - Spain

Order of Malta
established in the XII century under the Holy See
Local address: Pro Tantur - Hebron Road - P. O. B. 1763 – 91017 Jerusalem
Head Office: Palazzo Malta, Via Condotti, 68 - 00187 Roma - Italy

Personal Prelature of the Holy Cross and Opus Dei (Opus Dei)
established in 1982 under the Holy See
Local address: Gihon Street 11-B - 93547 Jerusalem
Head Office: 73 Viale Bruno Buozzi, - 00197 Rome - Italy

Pontifical Mission for Palestine
established in 1949 under the Holy See

Local address: New Gate - P.O.B. 19642 - 91196 Jerusalem
Head Office: 1011 First Avenue - New York, N.Y. 10022 - USA

Saint Thomas Foundation
established in 1989 under the Holy See
Local address: Shivtei Israel Road 8 - P. O. B. 298 - 97605 Jerusalem
Head Office: Secretariat of State, 00120 Vatican City

"Secours Catholique" (Caritas France)
established in 1946 under the French Bishops' Conference
Local address: Maison d'Abraham - Ras El'Amoud - P.O.B. 19680 - 91196 Jerusalem
Head Office: 106 rue du Bac - 75341 Paris Cedex 07 - France

Union of the Superiors of Women Religious of the Holy Land
established in 1993 under the Holy See
Shivtei Israel Road 8 - P.O.B. 298 - 97605 Jerusalem

Signed in _____ , this _____ day of the month of _____ in the
year _____, which corresponds to the _____ day of the month
of _____ in the year _____.

For the Holy See _____
For the Government of the State of Israel _____

The Schedule

(Article 12)

IMPLEMENTATION PROVISIONS

Pursuant to Article 12 of the "Legal Personality Agreement" (hereinafter: the "Agreement"), the following shall be its Implementation Provisions:

1. The application of the relevant provision of the Agreement to legal persons as are referred to in Article 3 § 1 (d) and Article 5, being new in Israel, shall be in accordance with the following sub-provisions:

1.1 (a) In this Provision, the term "pontifical" refers to ecclesiastical legal persons established by the Holy See, including their parts when they too are legal persons.

(b) Where a pontifical legal person has been established, and the Holy See intends that it function in Israel, a Certificate to that effect will be made by the Apostolic Nunciature in Israel. The Certificate will be delivered through the Ministry of Foreign Affairs to the Government of the State of Israel.

(c) The legal personality of the said pontifical legal person shall have full effect in Israeli law on the date of the conveyance of the Certificate by the Government to the Registry, described in Provision 5 or from the ninety-first day after the said delivery by the Nunciature — whichever is the earlier.

1.2 Where an ecclesiastical legal person other than a pontifical one has been established, and it is intended that it function in Israel, a Certificate to that effect will be made by the Authority that has established it, being either a Patriarch or a Diocesan Bishop, as the case may be, subject to the following sections:

(a) The Certificate will be delivered by that Authority or on its behalf through the Registry, described in Provision 5, to the Government of the State of Israel.

(b) (i) With reference to Article 3 § 2 of the "Fundamental Agreement", the Government of the State of Israel may request a discussion on the matter with the said ecclesiastical Authority on a mutually agreed level.

(ii) The discussion will take place in a bilateral committee consisting of an equal number of members from each side.

191

(c) Where such a discussion is not requested, or where agreement has been reached in the aforesaid committee, the legal personality of the said ecclesiastical legal person shall have full effect in Israeli law from the ninety-first day after the delivery of the aforementioned Certificate to the Registry or from the date of the agreement in the said committee, as the case may be.

(d) The above section (b) will not apply to Dioceses.

2.1 A merger of two or more legal persons to which the Agreement applies will have full effect in Israeli law after compliance with the following sections:

(a) If the Authority that has decreed the merger is the Holy See, a Certificate to that effect will be delivered by the Apostolic Nunciature in Israel, through the Ministry of Foreign Affairs, to the Government of the State of Israel.

(b) If the Authority that has decreed the merger is an ecclesiastical Authority other than the Holy See:

(i) that Authority will deliver a Certificate to that effect to the Registry.

(ii) The Holy See will issue a written Notice to be delivered by the Apostolic Nunciature in Israel in the manner described in section (a) to the effect that the contents of the Certificate are no longer subject to any appeal or recourse to any ecclesiastical forum. The Government shall convey this Notice to the Registry.

(c) The Certificates and the Notice referred to in sections (a) and (b) shall give the names of the two or more merged legal persons, the name of the new legal person, as well as all the other details referred to in Provision 5.3 of each of the merged legal persons and of the new one.

2.2 In case of a merger of two or more legal persons referred to in sub-provision 2.1 (a) or (b), the liability for outstanding obligations other than to ecclesiastical legal persons, whether being legal persons in accordance with the Agreement or not, shall be of the new merged legal person.

2.3 The date on which a merger referred to in sub-provision 2.1 (a) will have full effect in Israeli law shall be the ninety-first day from the delivery of the said Certificate to the Government, or from the date of its conveyance by the Government to the Registry — whichever is the earlier.

2.4 The date on which a merger referred to in sub-provision 2.1 (b) will have full effect in Israeli law shall be the ninety-first day from the delivery of the said Notice, through the Ministry of Foreign Affairs, to the Government, or from the date of its conveyance by the Government to the Registry — whichever is the earlier.

3.1 A dissolution of a legal person to which the Agreement applies will have full effect in Israeli law after compliance with the following sections:

(a) Liability for outstanding debts or other obligations of the dissolved legal person other than to ecclesiastical legal persons, whether being legal persons in Israeli law or not, shall be of the legal person that had established it as named in accordance with sections (b) (iii) or (c) (ii) below.

(b) if the Authority that has decreed the dissolution is the Holy See: (i) sub-provisions 2.1 (a) and 2.3 will apply; (ii) "dissolution" will be substituted for "merger";

(iii) the name of the legal person that had established the dissolved legal person will be included in the said Certificate together with the appropriate details related thereto as mentioned in Provision 5.3.

(c) If the Authority that has decreed the dissolution is an ecclesiastical Authority other than the Holy See:

(i) sub-provisions 2. 1 (b) and 2.4 will apply;

(ii) sections (b) (ii) and (iii) will apply to both Certificate and Notice.

3.2 Without derogating from sub-provision 3.1. outstanding debts or other obligations of the dissolved legal person to others who are not ecclesiastical legal persons, whether being legal persons in Israeli law or not, shall take precedence.

4. The Government of the State of Israel may, if in doubt, request the Apostolic Nunciature in Israel to verify an ecclesiastical document.

5.1 The Government of the State of Israel will establish a Registry for the recording of the following:

(a) documents communicated to the Registry under the Agreement;

(b) such documents as the Holy See or the Government of the State of Israel, or any legal person to which the Agreement applies, may cause to be communicated thereto.

5.2 The Registry shall be open to public inspection and copies authenticated by the Registry or by a notary or advocate licensed to practice in Israel shall be made available.

5.3 (a) The Register entry for any new legal person will include its official name, a local address and, if its head office is abroad, also its address, the name of its head or presiding officer, the date of its establishment by the Catholic Church and the ecclesiastical Authority that established it.

(b) In the case of a Diocese, the Register entry will also include a map showing its territorial jurisdiction.

5.4 Changes in details included in documents recorded under sub-provisions 5.1 and 5.3 (a) will be communicated and recorded in the same manner.

5.5 Documents recorded in the Registry will be prima facie evidence of their contents on the date of the document.

5.6 For the avoidance of doubt, none of the above sub-provisions shall be construed as derogating from any provision in Article 6 of the Agreement.

6.1 The Government of the State of Israel states that, in its opinion, the execution of provisions of this Agreement under Israeli law will require primary and secondary legislation. The Government agrees that the said secondary legislation will be made with the consent of the Holy See.

6.2 For the purposes of the legislation referred to in sub-provision 6.1, the Hebrew text of the Agreement shall prevail.

Signed in Jerusalem, this 10th day of the month of November in the year 1997, which corresponds to the 10th day of the month of Heshvan, in the year 5758.

_____   _____

For the Holy See   For the Government of the State of Israel

Basic Agreement Between the Holy See and
the Palestine Liberation Organization

Preamble

The Holy See, the Sovereign Authority of the Catholic Church, and the Palestine Liberation Organization (hereinafter: PLO), the Representative of the Palestinian People working for the benefit and on behalf of the Palestinian Authority:

Deeply aware of the special significance of the Holy Land, which is inter alia a privileged space for inter-religious dialogue between the followers of the three monotheistic religions;

Having reviewed the history and development of the relations between the Holy See and the Palestinian People, including the working contacts and the subsequent establishment — on October 26, 1994 — of official relations between the Holy See and the PLO;

Recalling and confirming the establishment of the Bilateral Permanent Working Commission to identify, study and address issues of common interest between the two Parties;

Reaffirming the need to achieve a just and comprehensive peace in the Middle East, so that all its nations live as good neighbours and work together to achieve development and prosperity for the entire region and all its inhabitants;

Calling for a peaceful solution of the Palestinian-Israeli conflict, which would realize the inalienable national legitimate rights and aspirations of the Palestinian People, to be reached through negotiation and agreement, in order to ensure peace and security for all peoples of the region on the basis of international law, relevant United Nations and its Security Council resolutions, justice and equity;

Declaring that an equitable solution for the issue of Jerusalem, based on international resolutions, is fundamental for a just and lasting peace in the Middle East, and that unilateral decisions and actions altering the specific character and status of Jerusalem are morally and legally unacceptable;

Calling, therefore, for a special statute for Jerusalem, internationally guaranteed, which should safeguard the following:

a) Freedom of religion and conscience for all.

b) The equality before the law of the three monotheistic religions and their institutions and followers in the City.

c) The proper identity and sacred character of the City and its universally significant, religious and cultural heritage.

d) The Holy Places, the freedom of access to them and of worship in them.

e) The Regime of "Status Quo" in those Holy Places where it applies;

Recognizing that Palestinians, irrespective of their religious affiliation, are equal members of Palestinian society;

Concluding that the achievements of the aforementioned Bilateral Permanent Working Commission now amount to appropriate matter for a first and Basic Agreement, which should provide a solid and lasting foundation for the continued development of their present and future relations, and for the furtherance of the Commission's ongoing task,

Agree on the following Articles:

ART. 1 — 1. The PLO affirms its permanent commitment to uphold and observe the human right to freedom of religion and conscience, as stated in the Universal Declaration of Human Rights and in other international instruments relative to its application.

2. The Holy See affirms the commitment of the Catholic Church to support this right and states once more the respect that the Catholic Church has for the followers of other religions.

ART. 2 — 1. The Parties are committed to appropriate cooperation in promoting respect for human rights, individual and collective, in combating all forms of discrimination and threats to human life and dignity, as well as to the promotion of understanding and harmony between nations and communities.

2. The Parties will continue to encourage inter-religious dialogue for the promotion of better understanding between people of different religions.

ART. 3 — The PLO will ensure and protect in Palestinian Law the equality of human and civil rights of all citizens, including specifically, inter alia, their freedom from discrimination, individually or collectively, on the ground of religious affiliation, belief or practice.

ART. 4 — The regime of the "Status Quo" will be maintained and observed in those Christian Holy Places where it applies.

ART. 5 — The PLO recognizes the freedom of the Catholic Church to exercise her rights to carry out, through the necessary means, her functions and traditions, such as those that are spiritual, religious, moral, charitable, educational and cultural.

ART. 6 — The PLO recognizes the rights of the Catholic Church in economic, legal and fiscal matters: these rights being exercised in harmony with the rights of the Palestinian authorities in these fields.

ART. 7 — Full effect will be given in Palestinian Law to the legal personality of the Catholic Church and of the canonical legal persons.

ART. 8 — The provisions of this Agreement are without prejudice to any agreement hitherto in force between either Party and any other party.

ART. 9 — The Bilateral Permanent Working Commission, in accordance with such instructions as may be given by the respective Authorities of the two Parties, may propose further ways to address items of this Agreement.

ART. 10 — Should any controversy arise regarding the interpretation or the application of provisions of the present Agreement, the Parties will resolve it by way of mutual consultation.

ART. 11 — Done in two original copies in the English and Arabic languages, both texts being equally authentic. In case of divergency, the English text shall prevail.

ART. 12 — This Agreement shall enter into force from the moment of its signature by the two Parties.

Signed in the Vatican, fifteenth of February, 2000.

Index

Index